In the FOOTSTEPS *of* ANNE

A JOURNEY THROUGH AVONLEA

ELIZA WESTFIELD

BOAT NOOK
PRESS

CONTENTS

My life is a perfect graveyard of buried hopes.

–ANNE SHIRLEY

INTRODUCTION

Despite her earlier hardships, Anne Shirley's life was anything but a graveyard once she arrived in Avonlea. Her creator, Lucy Maud Montgomery, had grand plans for this spirited, red-haired orphan who longed to be "beautiful" and free of freckles and fiery locks. Through Anne, Montgomery wove a tale of transformation, resilience, and the boundless possibilities of imagination.

Her Anne of Green Gables books provide a rich source of inspiration for girls and women alike to unpack their dreams, unfettered by social convention. Montgomery brought her protagonist to life in the early 20th century, an exciting time when feminist ideas were gaining popularity as more women fought for equal political rights and access to education (*Feminism in the 19th Century*, 2016).

While there were remarkable women in earlier centuries who made great strides in their respective vocations, the 20th century promised more change for women. Anne embodied this change, conveying a strong message that the time had come to be feisty! She was also very charming and made friends easily with wild geese, cherry blossoms, and kindred spirits.

Lucy Maud Montgomery: Prince Edward Island's Storyteller

Like Anne, Lucy Maud Montgomery was a trailblazer, a woman who challenged the status quo of her time. She was born on November 30th, 1874, in Clifton on Prince Edward Island (PEI), and she died on April 24th, 1942, in Toronto. Like many fiction authors, the places she described in *Anne of Green Gables* were very much a part of her own life. She was immersed in the beauty that greeted her in PEI and is undoubtedly Canada's most beloved author.

Montgomery's books are widely read worldwide. She remains a strong drawcard for tourists, all keen to learn more about her life, challenges, triumphs, and feminist beliefs. Ambitions like gaining a strong footing as a female writer were quite uncommon in the early 20th century. However, she was not discouraged; like Anne, Montgomery strongly desired to succeed. Her struggles are a testament to her courage, determination, and passion for writing.

As she wrote in one of her journals, "I cannot remember a time when I was not writing" (McIntosh & Devereux, 2013). The Anne books especially championed progressive ideas, with a central theme being *pursuing one's dreams*. This principle largely guided feminism in the early 20th century. It was all about breaking free from the chains of long outdated patriarchal values that had confined women to the role of wives and limited their career opportunities.

Lucy Maud Montgomery always wanted to be a writer, and so she did exactly that. *Anne of Green Gables* is hailed as one of her greatest literary accomplishments, and so it's safe to say Lucy did not give up easily on this pursuit. It was her first novel, published in 1908, and it instantly became a bestseller, resulting in immediate fame for Montgomery. In total, she produced 21 novels and more than 500 short stories.

Her literary accomplishments also include two poetry collections, numerous essays, and multiple journal anthologies. It is estimated that Lucy Maud Montgomery has sold 50 million copies of her work worldwide (McIntosh & Devereux, 2013). Since its publication, *Anne of Green Gables* has been immortalized in various television adaptations, which have won over many a heart and deepened interest in both Anne and Montgomery's accomplishments worldwide.

Unlike Anne, Montgomery came from a wealthy background. Her ancestors were well-educated and originally from Scotland, holding high positions in public office, which distinguished them by 18th- and 19th-century standards. Lucy, however, grew up feeling like an orphan as her mother died when she was just two years old. Not long after her death, her father remarried and moved on with his life. This created distance between them, leaving Montgomery mainly in the care of her grandparents in Cavendish, PEI.

She did not receive much affection from her grandparents and, like Anne, coped with her loneliness by reading and writing. One can almost imagine that some scenes in her Anne books are entirely guided by her adolescent fantasies. Indeed, Anne Shirley and Lucy Maud Montgomery are kindred spirits in many ways; both draw inspiration from the natural beauty of Avonlea and PEI at large.

The Enchanting Setting of Anne of Green Gables

Both Green Gables and PEI in general serve as the central settings for the Anne of Green Gables book series, which is why they remain popular tourist destinations to this day. Especially during the summer, visitors flock to Cavendish, a location strongly associated with this beloved literary achievement. Here, you can visit both the Green Gables house and the place that Montgomery called home. The Green Gables house has been preserved as a museum since 1936. It stands in impeccable condition, presented just as it would have been in her numerous Anne books.

Visitors can also look forward to the stunning scenery that greets them: the landscapes, beaches, and cultural heritage sites. PEI is warm in the summer, making it a perfect holiday retreat for the entire family. As you may have gathered by now, the idea behind this book in your hands is to recreate the beauty and magic that Anne discovered herself in Avonlea and PEI. I hope to encourage tourists to walk in her footsteps and truly connect with both Anne and her creator, Lucy Maud Montgomery, in the many pages to come.

Their determined and imaginative spirits live on in Cavendish and many other places in PEI. If you're an Anne fan, you will recall vivid scenes from the books or television adaptations, such as the excitement she felt when she stepped onto the shores of Avonlea or the trepidation she experienced at her first picnic by the *Lake of Shining Waters*. I'm sure you get it—for every Anne and Lucy fan, visiting PEI would be an absolute joy.

So, without further ado, I warmly welcome you on this amazing journey to PEI and the places that inspired Montgomery's enchanting community of Avonlea. As you explore, you'll discover fascinating insights into the world of Anne Shirley Cuthbert and the brilliant author who brought her to life. The next time you watch *Anne of Green Gables*, you'll appreciate it through a deeper, richer lens. Many more television adaptations of the spirited Anne, who cherishes kindred spirits and wears puffed sleeves, are sure to follow!

During your visit, you can look forward to a variety of outdoor activities, such as soaking in the stunning coastal scenery. PEI is renowned for its sandy beaches, perfect for hiking, cycling, and swimming. You'll also have the chance to learn about its iconic lighthouses, and it's a must to savor the seafood on the island, especially mussels and oysters. If you enjoy golfing or kayaking, you won't be disappointed either. Throughout the year, lively festivals take place here, and you can explore charming small towns and art galleries, along with meeting warm, welcoming locals!

Whether you are planning a trip to PEI, seeking a deeper appreciation of Montgomery's work, or simply revisiting the magic of *Anne of Green Gables*, this guide is here to offer something for everyone. Ultimately, it celebrates the enduring legacy of Anne Shirley Cuthbert and the stunning landscapes that inspired her remarkable story!

I read in a book once that a rose by any other name would smell as sweet, but I've never been able to believe it. I don't believe a rose WOULD be as nice if it was called a thistle or a skunk cabbage.

–ANNE SHIRLEY

Chapter 1

The World of Avonlea

Every story has a beginning. The first character we meet in *Anne of Green Gables* is Mrs. Rachel Lynde. We meet her when her peace is disrupted by the uncharacteristic behavior of Matthew Cuthbert. Seeing Matthew all dressed up in a white collar and heading out of town in his buggy piques her neighborly curiosity. It is too much for her to bear—being kept in the dark about the affairs of Matthew and Marilla Cuthbert, a pair of siblings who inherited Green Gables from their parents. They prefer to live quietly in their farmhouse, which is primarily surrounded by trees.

When she sees Matthew drive by, Rachel Lynde does what any decent inquisitive neighbor would do: she heads over to Green Gables right away! The purpose of her visit is to demand to know what is going on and where Matthew is going. Rachel is a walking encyclopedia of knowledge when it comes to everyone else's business in Avonlea. If there is a secret stirring in the village, Rachel will sniff it out faster than a foxhound on a scent.

But her heart is in the right place, and she is a somewhat comforting presence to have around, even if she leaves one spluttering for words—just as she does when she first meets Anne shortly after she arrives at Green Gables. Rachel has a deep love for the community of Avonlea, even if her words are sometimes brisk. In typical small-town neighborly hospitality, Rachel is always the first to bring a casserole in times of trouble and the loudest to cheer at church picnics. To the Cuthberts, Rachel is a loyal and steadfast friend. Her presence remains meaningful, humorous, and significant throughout the Anne books.

Needless to say, the opening scene of Anne of Green Gables is warm and inviting, keeping all its first-time readers hooked, as well as guessing what Matthew is up to on that fine day instead of planting turnips, as he said he would. That's because Matthew has other plans, as we soon discover—to fetch Anne from the Bright River train station. Upon his arrival, he is surprised to learn from the station master that a girl is waiting for him outside—not an orphaned boy as Matthew and Marilla had wished for.

Anne's personality immediately comes to life when she meets Matthew. We find her sitting outside, waiting patiently for him while making plans in her mind to sleep in the cherry tree down by the tracks if he does not show up. After all, it would be quite an adventure to sleep in a cherry tree, we later learn from Anne. We also discover that she did not want to sit and wait for Matthew in the ladies' waiting room because being outside offered greater scope for her imagination.

Immediately, readers are drawn to Anne's sense of adventure, love for nature, and the beauty of Avonlea!

Avonlea and Its Importance in the Stories

The colorful people of Avonlea lived a simple, rural life, but not without some excitement, drama, and tragedy woven in between. Anne certainly caused a stir upon her arrival. As much as Avonlea is real to its inhabitants—and to Anne fans—it is a fictional village. Situated on a triangular peninsula jutting out into the Gulf of Saint Lawrence, Avonlea is an enchanting town depicted as a close-knit community on Prince Edward Island (Montgomery, 1908).

Upon Anne's arrival, we also discover a lined avenue of blooming apple trees that are considered historic by Avonlea's standards. They were planted a long time ago. This avenue took Anne's breath away, so much so that she stopped talking completely to soak in the natural beauty and fully immerse herself in the scene.

Indeed, Avonlea is as beautiful as one can imagine from the pages of the Anne books, and it is where Green Gables, home to the Cuthberts, is located. The good news is that one does not need to be disappointed that Avonlea is a fictional village; its inspiration is deeply rooted in the real village life of Cavendish in the late 19th and early 20th centuries. As we touched on earlier, the town's creator, Lucy Maud Montgomery, grew up in Cavendish, which is located on the north shore of PEI.

In Avonlea, you will discover blooming orchards and many cherry trees. As Anne passed by the Avenue with Matthew, she exclaimed with glee that it should rightly be called *The White Way of Delight*. Anne enjoyed renaming places to capture their true beauty and essence. She famously renamed Barry's Pond to the "Lake of Shining Waters" because it felt right and gave her a thrill. She dutifully informed Matthew that she knew she had chosen the right name when it excited her, and so the Lake of Shining Waters remains one of the most famous attractions to discover in Cavendish.

Barry's Pond was named after Mr. Barry, who lived by it, and whose daughter, Diana, would become Anne's best friend. In fact, they would be bosom friends for life, just as Anne had romanticized. Anne's childhood and adult life certainly center around the main community of Avonlea, where she meets many kindred spirits. This makes Avonlea a dear place for her.

The Connection Between Avonlea and Cavendish

The serene rural community life we cherish in Avonlea mirrors that of Cavendish at that time, along with the landscapes and atmosphere. Montgomery drew extensive inspiration from her immediate surroundings, incorporating the red sandstone cliffs that still greet tourists today, as well as the pristine beaches and lush, rolling green fields—all of which have become key features of the beloved scenery that attract visitors to PEI.

The colorful characters in Avonlea reflect her real-life experiences growing up in a rural village. Charming farmhouses line the main road of Avonlea, while Green Gables is more isolated, situated at the farthest end of the cleared field on which it was built. This isolation was a source of dismay for Rachel Lynde, who could not understand why anyone would prefer to gaze at trees and remain somewhat distanced from the main road and neighborhood.

The Cuthberts loved their privacy and trees, and they were content with their quiet lifestyle on the farm. Still, they became more connected to the local community after Anne arrived. When Anne makes Green Gables her home, it becomes the centerpiece of her life in Avonlea. She falls completely in love with it, expressing gratitude for Octobers as she reflects on the beauty of the season and the natural world that surrounds her.

The flowering lanes, the glistening waters of the Lake of Shining Waters, the overarching apple trees of the White Way of Delight, as well as the bright woods all become part of her as she uses her imagination to give Avonlea an almost magical quality. Upon her arrival, we learn that there is a brook close to Green Gables. For Anne, discovering the brook made her first encounter with Green Gables even more beautiful.

Much of Avonlea, with its natural beauty and charm, exceeded Anne's imagination, as she readily admitted that she was happy—so happy—to belong to such a beautiful place. She had to pinch herself several times on her first day to ensure that it was real and not just another buried hope in the graveyard of her life!

Real-Life Cavendish

The qualities described by Montgomery in *Anne of Green Gables* feel within reach for tourists who flock to Cavendish today. Visitors can explore the glistening waters of The Lake of Shining Waters or visit the Green Gables house, which resembles the one in the novels. It is a popular tourist destination and heritage site, despite Avonlea being fictional. Cavendish has retained much of its pastoral beauty from the past while still offering modern amenities for visitors.

Green Gables was not merely a product of Montgomery's imagination; it was a significant part of her childhood. The orchards, gardens, and brook all exist in Cavendish, much to the relief and delight of Anne's fans. Restaurants, hotels, and shops bustle with tourists year-round.

Cavendish is a harmonious blend of rural charm and contemporary comforts, creating a delightful combination of nostalgia for Anne fans as they explore Avonlea's real-life attractions. The town offers visitors a unique experience where the timeless beauty of its pastoral landscapes coexists with modern conveniences and vibrant cultural sites, as seen in the various *Anne of Green Gables* television adaptations.

Significant efforts have been made to preserve all sites connected to both Anne and Lucy Maud Montgomery. The foundations of the author's family home, gravesites, and nearby attractions like *Lover's Lane* and *The Haunted Wood* are all present, as described in her writings. These sites were a tangible part of Montgomery's life and of the lives of the residents of Cavendish during that era.

The site where the one-room school of Avonlea once stood has been marked for tourists. You will discover it as you stroll down The Haunted Wood from the Green Gables Heritage Place. This site represents the school that Montgomery attended as a child. It's amazing how an entire island can be transformed into a magical place when one has a vivid imagination. Even the locals have come up with imaginative ways of recreating the Anne experience.

Prince Edward Island

To provide greater context for the descriptions of Cavendish and Avonlea, one can refer to the map of PEI, which is the smallest province in Canada. It is often described as a jewel of natural beauty and historical significance—for justifiable reasons.

Consult a detailed map of the island to find the island highlights and Cavendish's location relative to key landmarks like North Rustico, New London, and the PEI National Park. These areas enhance our understanding of Avonlea's idyllic surroundings, where nature and community coexist harmoniously.

Once in Cavendish, one is captivated by the rolling farmland, the iconic red dirt roads that define Avonlea, and the weathered wooden farm fences. All of this evokes the magnificent setting of Montgomery's stories. *The Green Gables Heritage Place*, featuring its classic white house and verdant gardens, transports fans directly into Anne's world.

And just so you know—**here's how you can get to PEI:** You can travel via direct flights to Charlottetown Airport, or you can cross the bridge by road through New Brunswick. Another travel option is to take a ferry from Nova Scotia—a place you might recall as Anne's orphanage home before she arrived in Avonlea.

In the next chapter, we will venture to Green Gables so that you can marvel at how well-preserved and scrumptious it is!

There's such a lot of different Annes in me. I sometimes think that is why I'm such a troublesome person. If I was just the one Anne it would be ever so much more comfortable.

–ANNE SHIRLEY

Chapter 2
Welcome to Green Gables

Green Gables is a special place because this is where Anne experiences lasting personal growth. It becomes her anchor as she transforms from a wildflower into a cherry blossom herself, a beautiful and confident young woman ready to face the world!

At Green Gables, Anne finally feels like she belongs. As first-time readers, we arrive at Green Gables alongside Anne, where she encounters the curious glare of Marilla Cuthbert, who promptly reminds Matthew that Anne is not a boy and must therefore be returned to the orphanage.

This scene is perhaps the first heart-wrenching moment we experience in *Anne of Green Gables*, and it lingers with us throughout the story, making it all the more joyous to witness Anne's growth and transformation at Green Gables over the years. Anne not only transforms the mindset of Marilla and Matthew, but she also transforms Avonlea with her bold ideas, ambitions, and a strong desire to break free from the restrictions placed on women during that era.

Montgomery uses the character of Anne to critique narrow-minded thinking. By celebrating Anne's individuality and intellect, she highlights outdated ideas that no longer suit imaginative and intelligent girls and women. Most importantly, we learn how love can help a young woman blossom into her full potential, as evidenced by the love and support Anne receives from the Cuthberts after her adoption, and the acceptance and affection she receives from some of the locals, especially Diana Barry and Gilbert Blythe.

Green Gables therefore symbolizes all of this and so much more. Its rustic charm serves as a timeless reminder of simpler days, evoking a sense of comfort and familiarity. Over the years, efforts have been made to preserve the house and its surroundings to ensure they remain a faithful representation of the setting described in Montgomery's books.

You are in for quite a treat when you visit the Green Gables Heritage Place because no effort has been spared to maintain the original structure. Nearby, you will find modern amenities that ensure your comfort as a visiting tourist. However, at Green Gables, the historic charm has not been compromised, allowing you to step into the farmhouse that represents the very one in which Anne lived in the late 1800s.

The Green Gables Heritage Place

If you have ever wondered what a typical farmhouse of the late Victorian period looked like, Green Gables, as it stands today, represents it perfectly. The house exudes a surreal charm and has remained in its original location since its construction in 1831 by the Macneills of PEI (Green Gables Heritage Place, 2023).

The Green Gables Heritage Place is more than a historical landmark; it serves as a window to a long-forgotten era when 19th-century women still received limited encouragement and support to pursue the careers of their choice. Despite this, the era embodied a wholesome charm and a revolutionary spirit which Montgomery beautifully depicts in her beloved Anne books. We can also appreciate the element of truth that filters through her writings.

Green Gables is not entirely fictional. The charm and hominess of the place, along with its large barn and orchards, have always been present. Since her childhood, Montgomery enjoyed the scenery at Green Gables, even if the farmhouse was not actually named that. It was once home to her and, therefore, it was a beloved place. Her maternal grandparents lived there, as did her great-grandfather, William-Simpson Macneill, who built the first farmhouse on the plot in 1806, shortly after his marriage (*The House of Home*, 2022).

The Macneills, who were among the first settlers on the island, laid a sturdy foundation on the very site where the house stands today. Montgomery was a fourth-generation Macneill by birth and the last generation of the family to live in the house she referred to as Green Gables in her books. She lived there with her grandparents from the age of three until she moved out at 18 (from 1876 to 1890).

As Green Gables was for Anne, the Macneill Farm was a source of stability and comfort for Montgomery. Even though her grandparents were not very affectionate toward her, she still had fond memories of her days at the farm. She consoled herself with play and fantasy and developed a love for reading from the tender age of six. The Green Gables farmhouse symbolizes a rugged yet self-sufficient 19th-century lifestyle, one that Montgomery was familiar with, making it easy for her to convey that information in her books, reflecting that era of her life with authenticity.

Montgomery briefly lived with her father when she left the Macneill Farm in 1890, after which she spent the next seven years preparing for her teaching career. Before her grandfather died in 1911, and after leaving the Macneill Farm, she lived in several other places. Still, she remained close to the Macneills and often visited her cousins and grandparents. Every inch of Green Gables pays tribute to both her and Anne's beautiful life on the Macneill Farm. Her love for kindred spirits, nature, and the farm that would inspire Green Gables is interwoven throughout her Anne novels.

Visiting the Green Gables Heritage Place makes the experience even more compelling because it represents both Anne's and Montgomery's childhoods. The exterior and interior of the house were reconstructed to resemble the description of Green Gables from Montgomery's novels, while the gardens and orchards were part of the Macneill Farm and the everyday scenes that Montgomery cherished during her time there.

Currently, the Green Gables house is situated near an 18-hole golf course and a busy road. However, it will undoubtedly remain a landmark of PEI—and Canada as a whole—because of its association with *Anne of Green Gables*, Montgomery, and the MacNeills, all of which add to its historical significance. Here, buried hopes were unearthed and nurtured until they grew wings and soared beyond the horizons!

Who could ever forget the lessons that Montgomery teaches us through Anne Shirley? Mark Twain, the renowned American writer, remarked—quite rightly—that "Anne is the dearest and most lovable child in fiction since the immortal Alice of Wonderland" (Parks Canada, 2019).

More About the Macneills and Lucy Maud Montgomery

In the 1900s, the farmhouse was owned, as stated, by her cousins, the Macneills. It was common then to paint the gables green. So, when Montgomery finally wrote her first novel, *Anne of Green Gables* in 1908, the story was largely influenced by the location and scenery of the Macneill Farm.

During Montgomery's early childhood years living with her grandparents Alexander and Lucy Macneill, the farmhouse kitchen also served as the Cavendish Post Office, making the Macneill Farm the center of community life in Cavendish. It was also a very important part of Montgomery's emotional and imaginative world. During those days in the late 19th century, the post office was where people met to share ideas, discuss politics, and catch up on news and gossip.

It is believed that these gatherings are where Montgomery found inspiration for the characters she created in her novels. When her grandfather passed away, and she returned from her teaching post to Cavendish in 1911, Montgomery also took over the responsibilities of running the post office. One of the advantages of being an assistant postmistress was the writing material that was accessible to her.

In those days, writing material was expensive and not much of it could be found in the Macneill household, so she got into the habit of writing down her stories and poems on the back of official letter bills. Outside the house, nature also nourished Montgomery, and this is reflected in the character of Anne and her journals where she expresses her love for nature and her gardens. It was here at the Macneill property where Montgomery penned much of *Anne of Green Gables*, and after her grandfather's death, while she served as assistant postmistress to the Cavendish Post Office, she wrote the remaining sequels.

The peaceful, inspiring setting of the farm helped her further develop her ideas and it would serve as the place where she would complete many of her future novels. Today, visitors can tour the house, enjoy interactive exhibits, and wander through the grounds and surrounding area. As a visitor, you can also partake in special Anne programs where people dress up in the characters of the fictional townspeople of Avonlea, and put on a real show that, once again, takes everyone back to the late 19th and early 20th centuries, where girls wore pinafores to school, and when puffed sleeves were fashionable.

You can quite literally walk in the footsteps of Anne and Montgomery once you're at the Green Gables Heritage Place. It is operated by Parks Canada and they have done a fine job ensuring that visitors get the most out of their visit. The idyllic setting around Green Gables also propelled Montgomery to write about Lover's Lane and the Haunted Wood. These paths are accessible from the Green Gables grounds.

What Awaits You at Green Gables

In the wondrous place called Green Gables, the imagination of the young Anne Shirley Cuthbert stirs, and her curiosity is piqued regardless of what is going on in the minds of her neighbors. Green Gables reminds us of this because it was here that Anne also engaged in modern, thought-provoking conversations with Marilla and Matthew Cuthbert, challenging old-fashioned notions about women.

Anne was free-spirited, untouched by limitations that governed the choices many other girls and women subscribed to in Avonlea. At Green Gables, she thrived and was allowed to be herself completely. As one walks through her bedroom door, they are reminded of how Anne swirled around in Marilla's white wedding veil, imagining she was the epitome of elegance and romance.

Also from her bedroom, which overlooked the farm, she could reach out to touch a cherry blossom tree, which she referred to as the "Snow Queen." In its quiet rooms and sunlit gardens, Green Gables still whispers stories of resilience, independence, free-spiritedness, and love. Feminism is only a label given to free-spirits exploring their imagination, just as Anne did. That much we get immediately from Montgomery's brilliant storytelling!

Visitor Tips: Best Times to Visit, Ticketing, and Nearby Amenities

Prince Edward Island National Park has worked tirelessly to maintain the authenticity of the site, ensuring that you will have an enriching experience during your visit. They have done everything possible to guarantee that an authentic Green Gables adventure awaits you. The kitchen is snug and ready for Marilla to light the stove and prepare her lovely hot meals.

There is much to see and explore in Cavendish. Here are some helpful visitor tips to help you make the most of your time at Green Gables and the surrounding area:

Best Visiting Times

The most popular time to visit Green Gables is during the summer months from June to September. The weather is warm and inviting for island activities, and the gardens around the house are in full bloom, as are the nearby woods.

The peak holiday season typically begins in July and lasts until the end of August, leading to a surge of visitors to the island. If you prefer a quieter experience, you can still enjoy the pleasant weather with smaller crowds. In that case, consider visiting as early as June or during Anne's October—it's easy to see why she loved it!

Fall arrives in October in PEI, awash in color from the changing leaves, making this a particularly lovely time to visit Green Gables. The winding paths are perfect for cool walks, while the gardens and forests are ablaze with warm reds and oranges. It's an excellent time to enjoy fewer crowds and relax by the shimmering Lake of Shining Waters with a picnic basket.

Ticketing

There are some exciting options to explore when buying your entry tickets to Green Gables Heritage Place. For instance, you can purchase a single-entry ticket, which grants access to the Green Gables House and its grounds only. Alternatively, you can opt for multi-attraction tickets, allowing for a broader exploration of PEI. The choice is yours.

The multi-ticket option is particularly beneficial if you're traveling with a group and want to organize your holiday itinerary. However, whether you're traveling alone or with family, it's advisable to plan well in advance through the official Parks Canada website. This will make your trip more organized, leaving little room for second-guessing. You can purchase your tickets online or at the entrance.

Nearby Amenities

There are plenty of activities to keep you exploring the island. The Green Gables Heritage Place is an important cultural and historical site, but there's so much more awaiting you.

Cavendish offers many wonderful restaurants to whet your appetite, and the shops and accommodations are amazing too. You can easily spend an entire day exploring the region while tasting its delicacies.

You can choose from a variety of activities, including nature trails, picnics, and beautiful beaches. Furthermore, Prince Edward Island National Park offers scenic hiking and biking opportunities for outdoor enthusiasts. This is a fantastic way to explore more of the island's stunning coastline!

For fans of Anne and Montgomery, the Anne of Green Gables Museum in Park Corner is a must-visit. This museum is unique, as it is situated in the house where Montgomery's cousin once lived, who served as the model for Matthew Cuthbert.

So, you see, there's so much more still to unfold in the pages of this book. Stay tuned for more exploration!

Oh, it's delightful to have ambitions. I'm so glad I have such a lot. And there never seems to be any end to them, that's the best of it.

–ANNE SHIRLEY

Chapter 3

Key Locations in Avonlea

Anne's journey from being a wildflower to an intelligent, warm-hearted young woman was full of trials and tribulations. She faced the added challenge of fitting in at school and in the larger community due to her "orphan" status.

Anne demonstrates that the pain of not fitting in is a universal experience transcending time and space. However, she also teaches us that our differences do not necessarily define our potential. Together, these are two deeply important lessons for girls and women, especially during the era in which the book was written.

If there is anyone most girls would love to have as their bosom friend, it would be Anne. Fortunately, she meets her ideal friend,

Diana Barry, at the picnic at the Lake of Shining Waters. Later, when school begins, Anne and Diana connect on a deeper level, pledging their allegiance to one another as bosom friends. This friendship is crucial for Anne, as Diana's acceptance, love, and support truly nourish her like nothing else.

Much later in life, Anne finds even greater nourishment in her lifelong romance with Gilbert Blythe. Anne's character shows us that true strength isn't about avoiding mistakes but rather about how we face them with courage, honesty, and an unwavering sense of self. She encounters many new challenges in Avonlea and at school, which she did not initially anticipate, but she perseveres through them all brilliantly, teaching valuable lessons.

Her persistence pays off, and Anne eventually makes her debut as a teacher at the Avonlea School when she turns 16. We meet her in this role in *Anne of Avonlea*. It was her first paying job, one she approached with great enthusiasm. Still, readers can't help but reflect on the younger Anne, who faced awkwardness on her first day at school.

During this stage of her life, she meets new people in Avonlea. Matthew Cuthbert has passed away, and Rachel Lynde moves in with Marilla after the death of her husband. Much has changed for the Cuthberts and their neighbor, who now becomes part of Anne's family. True to her nature, Anne continues to experience misadventures intertwined with heartfelt moments.

Despite the initial setbacks that both she and Marilla face following Matthew's death, Anne moves on to pursue her dream of attending college with Gilbert, and this marks a new beginning and chapter in her life as a mature young woman.

The Avonlea Schoolhouse

In *Anne of Green Gables*, the schoolhouse represents a crucial point of transition for Anne, and this theme continues in *Anne of Avonlea*. She continues to grow personally and professionally here, as well as in her relationships with the people of Avonlea. It is, therefore, an important location in her life.

The schoolhouse in Montgomery's novels is not just a building for acquiring an education; it is a place for bonding, connecting to the larger community, and challenging outdated norms and beliefs. The Avonlea School also served as the printing press for the *Avonlea Gazette*, which the community looked forward to reading.

Anne transforms from an awkward orphan here, into a bright journalist and teacher, challenging Mr. Phillips, her former teacher who had his favorites and never liked Anne very much. Mr. Phillips appeared to turn his nose up to Anne, due to her past, as well as due to being an outsider to Avonlea at first. This does not completely interrupt her growth, but it does, however, dampen her initial school days.

Thankfully, Miss Stacey takes over, and this nourishes Anne's education and growth into a bright young woman. These scenes are well known to Anne fans which makes visiting Avonlea School all the more interesting. Today, the school is a historical heritage site situated in the fictional village of

Avonlea in Cavendish. It symbolizes a time when the education of girls was not regarded as a major priority, especially when compared to marrying a suitable husband.

Anne and some of her friends, however, challenged this norm and went on to pursue careers. It was not a struggle for Anne to convince the Cuthberts of the need to further her education, but it was unfortunately a challenge for Diana and others to convince their parents. All of this reminds us of the significant role this small schoolhouse played in Avonlea, especially for Anne.

Even though it was fictional, the Avonlea Schoolhouse was based on real-life schoolhouses that were common in rural Canada at that time. They were mainly one-room schoolhouses. Montgomery drew inspiration from this, along with her own experiences attending a one-room school in Cavendish. However, Montgomery's experience in school was somewhat different from Anne's. From her private journals, we learn that Montgomery did not have many friends in school. In reality, Cavendish was an isolated farming community in the late 19th century, so she had limited contact with children her own age. In Montgomery's own words, "This forced me to construct a world of fancy and imagination very different indeed from the world in which I lived" (Brecknell, 2024).

Coming back to Anne, the first time she steps into the schoolhouse as a teacher is a monumental event in her life. Her head is full of dreams but she carries the weight of a new nervousness—one that she is not familiar with and one that is different from the nervousness she encountered as a student. However, she is determined to prove herself worthy as a teacher, just as Miss Stacey did before her when she replaced Mr. Phillips. Once again, we observe how Montgomery weaves in the importance of women role models for young girls.

Ever since Miss Stacey's arrival, Anne had been deeply inspired by teaching as a profession. Miss Stacey represented independence and modernity for Anne, even though she raised many eyebrows in Avonlea. She gave Anne strength, fueling her ambition and love for learning. Today, the Avonlea Schoolhouse stands as a testament to the power of education and symbolizes transformation since the turn of the century.

The Lake of Shining Waters: A Place of Reflection and Romance

"The Lake of Shining Waters was blue, blue, blue—not the changeful blue of spring, nor the pale azure of summer, but a clear, steadfast, serene blue as if the water were past all modes and tenses of emotion and had settled down to a tranquillity unbroken by fickle dreams" (Montgomery, 1915).

For readers—and Anne and Montgomery, of course—the Lake of Shining Waters symbolizes so much. The descriptions in the book are vivid and breathtaking, inviting readers to an enchanting place, just as it was for Anne and her friends, as well as for Montgomery. This pond is situated close to the Campbell Homestead, the home of her uncle John Campbell, the man who inspired Matthew Cuthbert.

This is why the Lake of Shining Waters holds a special place in the hearts of her fans, both on PEI and around the world. Visitors flock here from far and wide to be married. It is a beautiful spot—made even more lovely by the timeless words of Anne Shirley Cuthbert and Lucy Maud Montgomery. It certainly invokes love and romance, especially when one considers the enduring love Anne shares with the Cuthberts, Diana, and Gilbert Blythe.

The pond, located in Park Corner, is smaller than one might guess. Perhaps that's because Anne used her imagination to lead us to believe it was as big as a lake. There is a small garden by the pond with benches and a gazebo, where couples host their marriage ceremonies (Williams, 2015). It's amazing to think how a pond which is referred to as a lake was brought to life by Anne, and remains a source of pride for PEI today.

Renaming the pond to the Lake of Shining Waters thrilled Anne, and today it continues to inspire joy in those who visit, especially those who travel great distances to exchange their sacred wedding vows. Anne would surely feel satisfied by the trail of inspiration she has left for others. The lake was dear to her because it symbolized a new beginning—away from the orphanage and the cruel foster homes that repeatedly reminded her she was not kin and therefore never truly belonged.

From the moment Anne stepped off the train at Bright River Station, she sensed a belonging to Avonlea. The Lake of Shining Waters offered not only beauty to her but also hope for a brighter future. This body of water therefore teaches us so much—most importantly about not giving up on one's dreams.

The White Way of Delight: A Path of Beauty and Joy

The White Way of Delight is perhaps one of the most magical and dreamlike locations in *Anne of Green Gables*. Anne renames it from simply "the Avenue," and though it only exists in the fictional Avonlea and does not have a real-life counterpart, it is a significant enough part of the story that one can imagine that it truly does exist. For Anne, it was such a sight to encounter that she became still, very still, as Matthew rode with her through it.

In the book, the White Way of Delight is described as a place of great beauty. Given how Montgomery describes it, it truly is—it's a pathway with tall flowering trees on either side of it, majestic with white blooms shimmering in the sunlight. This path, too, symbolizes a beautiful new start in life for Anne. It represents her dreams, hopes, and aspirations to truly belong in the world.

In reality, the White Way of Delight is thought to have been inspired by a stretch of flowering trees near the Green Gables house, somewhere closeby to where Montgomery may have walked during her childhood. The exact location of the White Way of Delight remains unclear. It's left to visitors to use their imagination to picture it closeby to Green Gables. There are many trails near Green Gables, rich with birch trees and stunning beauty, that can easily capture the essence of the White Way of Delight!

Visiting all three of these important sites allows visitors to walk in Anne's footsteps; reflect on her imagination, life, and lessons; and marvel at how wholesome life was in the late 19th century. Whether you're standing at the Avonlea School, gazing at the shimmering waters of the Lake of Shining Waters, or walking along a sunny, tree-lined pathway reminiscent of the White Way of Delight, these locations provide a deep sense of connection to the world of *Anne of Green Gables*.

In the next chapter, we will learn more about Anne's family life and the closest connections she made during her time in Avonlea.

I'm so glad I live in a world where there are Octobers.

–ANNE SHIRLEY

Chapter 4

The Beauty of Prince Edward Island

If we were all a little more like Anne, we would easily find joy in our surroundings! Anne's most enchanting quality was her ability to make things right again, especially when they were upsetting—like when she first arrived at Green Gables and faced rejection because she was a girl and not a boy.

Still, Anne made an effort to be cheerful the next morning. As they began their journey to Mrs. Spencer to return her to the orphanage, she promptly said to Marilla, "It's been my experience that you can nearly always enjoy things if you make up your mind firmly that you will" (Montgomery, n.d.). Though deeply hurt and disappointed at not being able to stay at Green Gables, Anne resolved to make the best of the journey to Mrs. Spencer's. With her spirit undimmed by sorrow, she embraced the ride with hopeful curiosity.

Earlier that morning, Anne noticed the cherry and apple trees in full bloom at Green Gables from her bedroom window. There were also lilac trees in the garden below, and their sweet scent drifted up through the open window and caught her breath. As described in the novel itself, "The garden sloped down to the hollow where the brook ran" (Montgomery, 1908). From Anne's bedroom window, she could see the big barns to the left of Green Gables and, in the distance, the sparkling waters of the sea.

Needless to say, Anne marveled at the beauty that greeted her that first morning at Green Gables. It was the most splendid sight she had ever encountered, and to this day, if you look out over Green Gables, you will be welcomed by this beautiful scenery. PEI is well known for its sprawling forests, breathtaking gardens, and rolling hills. The natural landscapes of PEI are well documented in Montgomery's writings, conveying her deep connection to the environment.

Through Anne's eyes and heart, we sense Montgomery's love for the landscapes of PEI and experience what it meant to live there. The trees and orchards that Montgomery described originated from the Macneill Farm's orchards. Indeed, all of this beauty belonged to the gardens and other surroundings of the Macneill Farm when she wrote *Anne of Green Gables*. In fact, the first few lines of the story were written on the Macneill Farm, where Anne's trees and orchards also originated.

Montgomery's maternal grandfather, Alexander Macneill, planted apple trees behind their house and named them after all their children (*The House of Home*, 2022). The Macneill Farm was a cherished place for Lucy, Anne, the Cuthberts, and the Macneill family alike. Montgomery's gable window, from which she wrote much of *Anne of Green Gables*, overlooked that enchanting view of apple trees, cherry blossoms, and lilac trees.

Like Anne, Montgomery spent a lot of time in the forests of Cavendish. It was there that she experienced true fulfillment and joy. The more you learn about Montgomery, the more you see how closely Anne mirrors her personality. The beaches and hills represented sacred spaces for her, where she sought nourishment and solace, just as Anne did. They both cherished time alone for reflection, imagination, and creativity.

Scenic Locations: Beaches, Forests, and Rolling Hills

The Beaches of Prince Edward Island

Like most people who live on the island, Anne loved the beach, and there's a lot of ocean to love when you're in PEI. In *Anne of Green Gables*, she spends time on the shores of the local beaches, enjoying the solitude as she reflects on her dreams. Canada's best beaches are found in PEI. From Green Gables itself, Cavendish Beach is not too far away. It is the most famous beach on the island because it is closely associated with Anne.

Cavendish Beach is a long stretch of sandy beach well known for its dramatic red sandstone cliffs. This feature appears in many television adaptations of *Anne of Green Gables* and is also referenced in the Anne books. There are not many beaches in the world defined by red sandstone cliffs, but Cavendish Beach certainly is. Basin Head Beach is another beach closely connected to Anne and Montgomery. It is located on the eastern shore of the island and is very popular with tourists.

The water is crystal clear, warm, and enticing. The sand on the beach is soft and wonderful to experience, especially if one spends many hours there. The view from the beach is spectacular, and nearby, there are excellent amenities to enjoy. But what makes this beach unique is its white singing sands. Yes, you read that correctly! The pristine white sands of Basin Head Beach are more than just a scenic marvel—they're a geological wonder.

When stepped on, the sand produces a distinctive "singing" sound, a phenomenon attributed to its exceptionally high silica content—a natural mineral found in sand, quartz, and various rocks. Its unique structure causes the sand grains at Basin Head

Beach to rub against each other in just the right way when compressed, producing a distinctive squeaking or "singing" sound. This rare feature has earned Basin Head Beach its enchanting nickname: "The Singing Beach."

Once there, you can explore the fisheries museum, which has become a popular tourist destination. There is also a safe play area for children, along with washroom and shower facilities.

The Forests of Prince Edward Island

Now, let's explore the enchanting forest tours on the island, which you are sure to love. You will undoubtedly be following in the footsteps of Anne and Montgomery, who both romanticized nature. Lucy wrote in her journal, on December 20th, 1908, "I am thankful above all else for my love of nature and my capacity for finding the fullness of joy in her companionship. I would rather lose everything else I possess than that" (Bode &

Mitchell, 2018). Anne therefore very much embodied Montgomery's spirit in many ways.

And you, too, will get that sense when you visit Green Gables Heritage Place. There, you must experience The Haunted Wood trail which both Anne and Montgomery enjoyed exploring. Walking through this forest is an absolute must. The tall trees and winding paths hold significance, as many scenes take place in these wooded areas of Cavendish. No doubt these are scenes that were very real for Montgomery. She made up the Haunted Wood trail with two "impish friends," Wellington and David Nelson.

These two boys believed in the existence of ghosts and they would often make up stories of hauntings to scare Montgomery with. It rubbed off on her too, and all three of them decided to declare a pretty spruce grove "The Haunted Wood." It was all play and fantasy, but eventually, their stories became so compelling that they avoided the Haunted Wood altogether at times out of fear of the things they imagined took place there (*The Haunted Wood Trail at Green Gables Heritage Place*, 2024).

Both Anne and Montgomery escape to the forests to process their emotions and withdraw from the pressures they face at times. From *Anne of Green Gables*, we learn how she loved losing herself to her imagination when she entered the woods. The Haunted Wood is filled with dark, towering trees (according to Anne) that can feel eerie, especially when one is alone. We can only conclude that it offered Anne much scope for the imagination!

In reality, the forests near Cavendish remain an integral part of the landscape, just as they were during Anne's and Montgomery's time in the late 19th and early 20th centuries. They remain largely untouched and extraordinary to explore, just as they did back then. The woods are filled with a variety of trees. If you're on a guided tour, you will learn more about the trees and how to differentiate between fir, pine, and spruce. These trees play an important role in the island's ecosystem.

To make the most of your forest adventures, you can access them via PEI's National Park. This way, you will discover many wooded trails that wind through forests and pristine beaches. If you're feeling particularly adventurous, you can also hike or enjoy a truly marvelous biking experience along those trails. The views are stunning, and these wooded paths offer the perfect opportunity to immerse oneself in the natural world of PEI.

Let's now delve into the hiking and biking trails awaiting your exploration, each offering its own unique adventure and scenic charm.

Hiking Trails

Here are the most popular areas for hiking. If you love hiking and nature like Anne and Lucy Maud, then you can spend some time exploring all of these wonderful trails!

- **Prince Edward Island National Park:** To make the most of your hiking adventure, head over to The Greenwich Interpretation Centre. There you will gain access to forest trails that wind through dunes and along the coastline as well. You can explore a mix of forested trails and beach walks. The Greenwich Dunes Trail is very popular because, as you could probably assume, you get to hike through the dunes. It's a relatively easy trail to follow which makes it accessible for all levels of hikers.

- **Bonshaw Hills Provincial Park:** Bonshaw Hills is located right in the heart of PEI, and it is known to offer some especially rugged trails for those seeking more adventure and forested hiking. It offers a peaceful escape and unique views of PEI.
- **The Confederation Trail:** This is an absolute must because of its historic significance. It is very popular and scenic and follows the path of an old railway line that spans the length of the entire island. It passes through forests, wetlands, and rolling hills, offering stunning views all around. The trail is historic because it follows in the footsteps of Montgomery's characters. You will pass through small villages, including Cavendish and Avonlea. This trail is accessible for all levels of hikers.
- **The Green Gables Heritage Place Trails:** At this site, you can access more wonderful short hiking trails like the Haunted Wood Trail and Lover's Lane. It offers a unique experience because these locations inspired some of the most memorable scenes in *Anne of Green Gables*. You will also get to see the original spot of the one-room school that Montgomery attended via

The Haunted Wood trail. This school inspired the one-room Avonlea School that Anne attended. Apart from that, you will stop at the gravesite of Montgomery and her original Cavendish home, where she lived with her grandparents.

Biking Trails

There are glorious biking opportunities on the island. If you are interested in enjoying most of your outdoor time biking, then The Confederation Trail is the one for you. That's because it stretches for 435 miles, giving you a longer scenic trail. Since it was once a railway line, the route is mainly flat and smooth, making it perfect and easy for biking enthusiasts.

It also passes through very scenic locations, like wooded areas, villages, and iconic Montgomery spots. It is a great way to bike through nature as a tourist of PEI. Of course, there are other mountains and forested trails to explore on the island, apart from The Confederation trail. Places like the Bonshaw Hills Provincial Park and Brookvale Provincial Ski Park offer more rugged terrain. These trails are excellent choices for mountain biking.

Whatever suits you best, walking or biking, you are spoiled for choice on PEI because there is something for everyone to enjoy!

Exploring the Great Outdoors: Adventures Beyond Hiking and Biking

You can go kayaking; picnicking in the forests, valleys, or beaches; birdwatching in the wetlands and forests; or even horseback riding, sailing, or playing golf! There's an 18-hole golf course situated close to the Green Gables Heritage Place. All of these wonderful activities are set against the gorgeous backdrop of PEI's stunning landscapes.

PEI is also famous for its rolling hills and lush green fields. By immersing yourself in as many outdoor activities as possible, you will gain a firsthand glimpse of the magnitude of its beauty. It's no wonder Anne fell into despair when Marilla wanted to send her back to the orphanage; she knew that PEI offered her something truly magical. She was so happy to be in Avonlea, from the moment she got off the train.

PEI offers endless inspiration for the imagination, just as Anne once sensed. Simply create a list of your favorite activities and envision some unforgettable adventures. Then, let go, surrender to the wonders of nature, plot your tours, and immerse yourself fully in the enchanting beauty of Avonlea!

Kindred spirits are not so scarce as I used to think. It's splendid to find out there are so many of them in the world.

–ANNE SHIRLEY

Chapter 5
Anne's Friends and Family

As we delve into Anne's new world of Avonlea, we encounter a cast of unforgettable characters who captivate our imaginations, stir our emotions, and leave lasting impressions. Each character adds charm and depth to *Anne of Green Gables*, presenting us with universal themes, such as friendship, love, resilience, rejection, societal pressure, faith, and transformation.

However, we still feel tension as we discover Marilla's stern disapproval of Anne. This sets the stage for conflict whenever Anne gets into trouble. We often wonder how Marilla Cuthbert will react:

will she come to Anne's rescue, or will she be responsible for reprimanding her and regretting her decision to keep her?

Spurred on by Rachel Lynde's initial cautionary remarks about taking in an orphaned girl, Marilla harbors doubts and suspicions that their decision might lead to something dreadful. Marilla, therefore, represents both tension and transformation in the story. It is only after we get to know her a little bit more that we see through her outward stern demeanor.

At heart, we learn that Marilla is truly a kindred spirit to Anne, and our affection for her grows deeper throughout the book. She ultimately has Anne's best interests at heart, and it is her love and support for Anne that warms us. Marilla's love develops into motherly affection for Anne, as she often comes to her defense whenever Anne's presence draws contempt from others in Avonlea.

The Cuthberts and Montgomery's Grandparents

As we discover Marilla's transformation and growing devotion to Anne, it makes us wonder if Montgomery's grandmother may be likened to Marilla Cuthbert in some ways, given her strict Victorian-era beliefs about discipline, religion, and etiquette.

Sadly, this was not the case. Montgomery was a lonely child who did not receive any love or enjoy any closeness at all with her grandparents. Many say that Montgomery projected her fantasies onto Anne for love and approval.

Also, despite the stunning success of *Anne of Green Gables*, it did not cheer her up as much as she hoped it would. The happy endings she so vividly portrayed in her books remained elusive to her. Not only was Montgomery mainly unhappy in her childhood and marriage, but her professional life was also largely unfulfilling.

Indeed, even her successful literary career failed to lift the shadows that loomed over her life since the day she was born. Behind the veneer of success lay a reality that no amount of acclaim could truly erase.

In life, neither of her grandparents offered her any affection, nor were they transformed in any way by her gifts, whereas Anne's individuality appealed to both Matthew and Marilla Cuthbert. It grew on the Cuthberts, so much so that they were proud of Anne and stood up for her when others put her down.

One of the most memorable scenes of *Anne of Green Gables* is when Anne accidentally gets Diana Barry drunk on currant wine, mistaking it for raspberry cordial. Marilla sticks up for Anne when Diana's mother severs their friendship. Marilla always offers something nice to say about Anne when others put her down, without forgetting to remain respectful. This is one of Marilla's strongest and most appealing personality traits.

Anne's Family Life in Avonlea Versus Montgomery's Life in Cavendish

One can only feel sorry for Anne, who easily drew criticism and harsh judgment from the characters of Avonlea due to her orphan status. Thankfully, Marilla and Matthew offer her love, validation, and protection from continuous rebukes and disapproval. Similarly, Gilbert Blythe, her classmate, friend, and later husband provides her with validation and camaraderie when she is put down by others.

As mentioned earlier, Montgomery had few friends in her childhood and, unlike Anne, was offered no comfort at all. She faced ongoing disapproval from her grandfather. Anne, however, faced no disapproval from either Matthew or Marilla regarding her ambitions. They always supported her and wanted her to succeed.

Montgomery's grandfather did not believe that a woman should be educated; he succumbed to the prevailing belief of the times—namely that a woman's highest success was in obtaining a suitable husband. Matthew, on the other hand, admired Anne's imagination and encouraged her during difficult moments. He also urged her to attend Queen's Academy in Charlottetown to further her education, despite Marilla's initial reservations.

He stood up for Anne and never diminished her light or spark for creativity. Both Marilla and Matthew were open-minded regarding Anne's need for validation as an intelligent woman. Neither one of them imposed old-fashioned notions upon her young shoulders.

In life, Montgomery was not as lucky as Anne was when it came to gaining support from a father figure or a partner. Matthew and Gilbert, the two most important men in Anne's life, both embodied the qualities that Montgomery preferred in men—

gentle, supportive, and quietly steadfast, with respect for female intellect and individuality.

Sadly, those qualities remained absent in her husband who instead entertained darker delusions about religion and faith. Few personal details are known about Ewan Macdonald, the man Montgomery married, except that their marriage was overshadowed by his mental illness and delusions about them being doomed to hell as a family (Fasick, 2021).

It was when Montgomery's grandmother died in March 1911 that she married Macdonald. Her engagement to him was long. She compelled Macdonald to keep their engagement a secret until the death of her grandmother, which speaks volumes about her relationship with her grandmother. Many were surprised by their marriage as she announced it very suddenly, a few weeks after her grandmother's death.

Macdonald was a 40-year-old Presbyterian minister at the time of his marriage to Montgomery. They knew each other for five years before their marriage, and it was clear from Montgomery's journal entries that she did not love him as passionately as Anne loved Gilbert Blythe. Instead, it was a pragmatic choice for Montgomery, as she very much explained in her journal, "This is a practical world and marriage must share in its practicalities" (Brecknell, 2024).

Visits to Locations Relevant to Avonlea Characters

Matthew Cuthbert and Green Gables

Matthew Cuthbert was gentle and reserved yet supportive and loving toward Anne. These appealing traits helped maintain a calm atmosphere in the Cuthbert home at Green Gables. He served as an anchor of support for both Anne and Marilla and was deeply rooted in Green Gables like the ancient trees surrounding it. Dedicated to working on the farm and his family, he remained steadfast in his open-minded approach to Anne's imaginative ramblings.

Matthew was an enduring spirit, easy to like and get along with. He never had a harsh word to say about anyone and preferred to stick to familiar routines. Humble by nature and kind in his ways, his tenderness grew deeper and more beautiful over the years. He played the father figure in Anne's life with grace and ease, finding solace in the simplicity of life at Green Gables. He would take his tea at 4 p.m., help with household chores, and develop a keen interest in dresses with puffed sleeves.

Matthew's quiet strength and gentle support provided Anne with stability, validation, and confidence. He became her quiet sanctuary, lifting her when she felt overwhelmed by life's challenges. He was the first person with whom Anne bonded upon her arrival in Avonlea, and he was also the only one who never criticized her or argued with her about her fantasies. We witness his tenderness when he refrains from spoiling Anne's mood by telling her outright that she ought to have been a boy and not a girl orphan.

While Green Gables anchors him in routine and familiarity, Anne awakens in him a purpose long dormant—a life beyond hard work and solitary existence. He loves Anne instantly; this is evident as he fights for her to stay at Green Gables. Matthew is a true kindred spirit, as Anne rightfully remarked upon her arrival. He never missed a chance to support her or celebrate her accomplishments.

His gestures, though not grand, are simple while still meaningful and loving. Matthew's legacy lies in the land of Green Gables and the love and support he poured into Anne. It is this spirit of gentleness that ensures the essence of *Anne of Green Gables* endures in our hearts forever.

Marilla Cuthbert and the Avonlea Church

Marilla Cuthbert is a strong, straightforward, yet kind-hearted soul who brings warmth and stability to Anne. Green Gables is central to Marilla's life, just as it is to Matthew's, and her tradition and loyalty to her faith provide comfort not only to her family but also to the local community of Avonlea. Marilla embodies Christian values and chastises Anne at times for lying or avoiding her chores and responsibilities due to daydreaming.

She is also responsible for bringing both balance and harmony to Anne's life in her unique ways. Marilla steps immediately into a motherly role and directs Anne toward good neighborly conduct. She also teaches her about faith, God, and what it means to uphold good moral values in her choices. She encourages Anne and deeply respects her as a soul deserving of a good chance in life.

Marilla's unwavering support and love for Anne blossom over the years, just as they do for Matthew. She also develops a protective role in Anne's life, keeping her best interests in mind and at heart, especially when others unfairly criticize or judge her for her mistakes. With a practical, no-nonsense approach to life and raising Anne, Marilla often rebukes Matthew for being too soft on her and for giving in too easily to her whims and fancies.

Marilla tends to Green Gables and Anne efficiently. She is strong, orderly, and unyielding to frivolities. Yet, beneath her stern exterior, we once more see a kindred spirit, and we witness her capacity to experience profound love over the years. The place in Avonlea most dearly connected to Marilla is the whitewashed church of Avonlea. It is here that she reaffirms her values, morals, and faith. The church symbolizes her simplicity, strength, and devotion to Anne.

A visit to this church is an absolute must, as it symbolizes Marilla Cuthbert's dedication to the principles guiding her decisions. The fictional village of Avonlea is home to several heritage buildings, including the historic Long River Church. It was restored and relocated here so that Anne fans and residents could take pride in its heritage. Built in 1874, the Long River Church remains a steadfast symbol of community and faith (*Long River United Church*, 2024).

Diana Barry, Orchard Slope, and Barry's Pond

Besides the Cuthberts, there isn't any kindred soul in Avonlea more dear to Anne than Diana Barry. The contrast between their backgrounds does not impede their ongoing friendship. Just as Anne bonded with the Cuthberts and recognized their important place in her life, the same can be said for Diana Barry. Their friendship began to bloom on the first day of their encounter, at Anne's first picnic, by the Lake of Shining Waters.

Despite the initial caution displayed by Diana's parents, this friendship flourished for many years. Diana was a kindred spirit, despite her more privileged background. She was just as free-spirited as Anne was, and she was kind with a keen mindset on being educated further.

Orchard Slope was home to the Barrys. It is a picturesque estate that is a testament to Diana's privileged life. The estate itself is surrounded by orchards overlooking Anne's Lake of Shining Waters. Like Matthew and Marilla Cuthbert, Diana was a source of great comfort and love for Anne. Orchard's Slope was across the road from Green Gables, making it easy for both Anne and Diana to meet often and walk together.

Diana's friendship offers Anne the stability and reassurance she needs. Not all the kids in school were nice to her, but from the onset, Diana was very nice indeed. Her loyalty to Anne is truly inspiring, and despite her privileged upbringing, Diana embodies a maturity and humility that far exceed her years.

Therefore, the Lake of Shining Waters remains an enduring symbol of the love and friendship shared by Anne and Diana. Their carefree spirits live on here, mingling with the rustling leaves and the rippling water that sparkles beneath the sunlight.

Gilbert Blythe, Blythe Farm, and Avonlea Schoolhouse

The Blythe Farm offers a vivid glimpse into the hardworking rural life that shaped Gilbert Blythe's steadfast and admirable character. One cannot visit Blythe Farm except in one's imagination; however, it is important to note that this is where Gilbert found stability. The farm exists only in the fictional Avonlea, amid the rolling fields and hills, on the same road where Green Gables is situated. With the Macneill Farm as Green Gables' real-life stand-in, this should give you an idea of where the Blythe Farm would be.

Gilbert learned hard work on the farm, and discipline shaped his character, turning him into a witty and kind partner for Anne. Their journey began at the Avonlea School, where their destinies became intertwined, first as children and later as husband and wife. It is a remarkable love story that Montgomery wove into her Anne books, one that inspires friendship, spans decades, and is intertwined with the beauty of PEI.

This romance may reflect the love Montgomery herself craved. She is known to have experienced many crushes in the one-room school she attended in Cavendish, represented by an empty spot of land on the way to her gravesite today. In the fictional village of Avonlea, one can draw inspiration from the wonderful days of Anne and Gilbert and the rivalry they experienced in their earlier days. The schoolhouse that is in Avonlea Village is the actual schoolhouse that Lucy Maud Montgomery taught in, which makes this a remarkable heritage site.

One of the most famous scenes in the novel occurs when Gilbert teases Anne about her hair, calling her "Carrots" and provoking her temper. This, of course, leads to Anne breaking a slate over his head. However, this childish rivalry evolves into a dynamic friendship rooted in mutual admiration and respect. Today, as a tourist, you can visit the Avonlea School in the fictional village specifically set up for visitors.

The schoolhouse features slate blackboards and rows of wooden desks, all lined up neatly, just as they existed back in the 1870s when it is believed to have been first built. Here, children can gain insight into what schools were like in the late 19th century.

Furthermore, at the Avonlea Farm, kids can enjoy pony rides and get ice cream or straw hats, making it a fun outing!

In the next chapter, we will take a closer look at Lucy Maud Montgomery's Literary Trail so that you can make the most of your trip to Cavendish—and PEI as a whole!

We pay a price for everything we get or take in this world; and although ambitions are well worth having, they are not to be cheaply won.

–LUCY MAUD MONTGOMERY

Chapter 6
The Literary Trail

The one good thing Montgomery's grandmother did for her was encourage her to obtain an education, despite the narrow-mindedness of the era in which she lived. Indeed, Lucy Mcneill instructed Montgomery to respect the written word and approved of her spending time in nature.

It was a blessing of sorts because this was all that her grandmother ever really approved of when it came to Montgomery. Like her grandfather, Alexander, Lucy Macneill did not think much of her granddaughter's fanciful imaginings. They did not understand her nor did they like her playful ideas. We know this because Montgomery kept a journal from a young age, which also explains the richness of the characters she creates in her books.

Montgomery was not only imaginative and witty—in fact, she was also a deep thinker and very progressive in her private thoughts. Her writings in her journal were honest reflections of her true feelings. From her early journal entries, one can easily deduce—as historians have already—that Montgomery had a difficult and lonely childhood. Her spiritedness was a constant headache for her grandparents who favored instead that their granddaughter adhere to a strict code of conduct, following their Presbyterian lifestyle.

Except for the issue of education and nature, Montgomery had nothing else in common with her grandmother. This minimal encouragement was exactly what Montgomery needed, and so it served her well. In no time at all, she realized her passion for both reading and writing. At least, it was an occupation that did not raise her grandmother's eyebrows. And so at the tender age of 16, Montgomery published her first poem. It was titled "On Cape LeForce," and published in the Charlottetown newspaper, *The Daily Patriot* (*Poet Lucy Maud Montgomery Poems*, 2019).

She was very proud of this achievement and continued writing poetry. By the time she was 24, Montgomery had published 28 short stories, 46 poems, and 12 essays and a selection of sketches (Green, 2022). That said, her literary journey and rise to fame did not come easily. She learned the hard way that ambition alone did not guarantee success. Despite her passion for writing and countless attempts during the early days of her career, Montgomery struggled to gain the recognition she craved.

She identified herself as a writer before anything else, even before becoming a teacher. Writing was her true passion. There were limited opportunities for female writers back then, and this was part of her struggle to gain recognition. This is why Mongomery turned to teaching as her main profession. It was a choice of practicality rather than passion. Montgomery taught in three schools on the island. She also furthered her studies while teaching during this period. In between teaching, she took up her formal studies at Dalhousie University in Halifax, Nova Scotia.

A Look Into Montgomery's Professional Life

Montgomery's other job was working as an editor for a newspaper. Both her jobs were demanding and she was afraid of neglecting her main passion, which was still writing, of course. This prompted her to rise early every day so she could squeeze in an hour of writing before heading to work. Along the way, she faced bitter disappointments. "Only lonely people keep diaries," Montgomery once wrote in her private journal. This was quite revealing of the true reality of her situation. We also learn from her journals that she became quite adept at putting on a cheerful front for others, even though deep inside she was lonely and unhappy.

By 1903, Montgomery wrote that she was "tired of existence and practically alone in the world." In her words, "Soon youth will be gone and I shall have to face a drab, solitary, struggling middle age. It is not a pleasant prospect" (Brecknell, 2024). Montgomery's search for meaning in life was mainly tied to her writing, yet it eluded her for many years. Finally, one day inspiration bloomed. In her log book, where she jotted down ideas for writing, she wrote, "Elderly couple apply to orphan asylum for a boy. By mistake, a girl is sent them" (Brecknell, 2024)

That entry marked the beginning of Montgomery's most enduring character, Anne Shirley. Due to the challenges Montgomery faced, both personal and professional, she did not achieve success instantaneously. It was a painstaking and somewhat harrowing journey for her to finally get her first novel published. Initially, she sent the manuscript to five different publishers. All of them rejected *Anne of Green Gables*. Facing this bitter disappointment, Montgomery decided to put Anne away in an old hat box.

Two years later, after rereading the manuscript, she gave it another try, and to her utter amazement and joy, *Anne of Green Gables* was finally published by L. C. Page & Company of Boston. It hit the shelves of bookstores in June 1908. Given the many setbacks she faced in life, it was deeply rewarding when she finally held a printed copy of *Anne of Green Gables* in her hands. She received praise from many reviewers. One of them wrote, "The book radiates happiness and optimism."

This delighted Montgomery and she subsequently wrote in her journal, "When I think of the conditions of worry and gloom and care under which it was written I wonder at this" (Brecknell, 2024). But her happiness was only momentary. There were many battles ahead of her, which included one with the aforementioned publisher, L. C. Page. They demanded full rights to the book (Fasick, 2021). After a lengthy legal battle, which lasted many years, Montgomery finally won her legal suits against Page in 1928.

Reflecting on her struggles in this legal journal, Montgomery wrote, "Sometimes I almost give up in despair, but I cannot. I will keep on—struggling and hoping (Brecknell, 2024)." Strangely, her success with *Anne of Green Gables* was a bit overwhelming for her. When Montgomery finally got what she desired, the recognition she craved, she became tired of Anne. After writing *Anne of Avonlea,* she remarked in her journal that she should "bitterly repent" for creating the character of Anne Shirley.

Even though Montgomery did not realize it then, the sequels were important to the Anne series, adding more depth to her talent and carefully woven story and characters. Montgomery was mainly spurred on by her second publisher to write the sequels to her Anne books, especially the ones that followed *Anne of Avonlea*. In 1922, Montgomery confessed that she liked her new character, Emily Byrd Starr, more than Anne and that her book, *Emily of New Moon*, was the best book she had ever written.

Emily was also an orphan girl, but she was not as optimistic as Anne. Perhaps the hard knocks of life were finally getting to Montgomery who sought comfort in her new complex character, Emily. Montgomery went on to write two sequels to *Emily of New Moon—Emily Climbs* and *Emily's Quest.* Her final novel, *Jane of Lantern Hill*, was written and published in 1937. Five years later, Montgomery died at the age of 67.

Celebrating a Woman Who Was Passionate About Reading and Writing

To truly celebrate Montgomery's enduring legacy, one must start at the very beginning of her journey. It all began in Clifton, PEI, where Lucy Maud Montgomery was born on November 30th, 1875. Now known as New London, her birthplace is a historic site and a popular destination for fans of her work.

You will enjoy spending time soaking in the pastoral beauty of New London. Its emerald pastures stretch toward the horizon, promising new beginnings. The rocking boats evoke memories of simpler days and beautiful dreams. Despite its dreaminess, though, Clifton was not all that Montgomerys hoped it would be. Her joy there was short-lived.

Clara Woolner Macneill, Montgomery's mother, died at the young age of 23 from tuberculosis. The year was 1876, and Montgomery was 21 months old. Despite her tender age, Montgomery claims her earliest memory of her mother is seeing her in her coffin.

Montgomery recalls not feeling sorrow when her mother died. She famously said, "I was only vaguely troubled. Why was Mother so still? And why was Father crying? I reached down and laid my baby hand against Mother's cheek. I could feel the coldness of that touch" (McIntosh et al., 2013).

Shortly after her mother's death, her father, Hugh John Montgomery, gave full custody of Montgomery to her maternal grandparents. He was stricken with grief and unable to cope with a child. This left Montgomery without either parent present in her upbringing.

A Guide to Locations Significant to Lucy Maud Montgomery's Life

Visiting Montgomery's birthplace is a remarkable opportunity. At the modest green and white house overlooking New London Harbour, you will learn more about Montgomery's first months in

PEI. Her literary trail is an absolute must on your tourism list. It includes wonderful and significant sites linked to her life.

As you explore these sites, you may come to realize, as many others have, that visiting these sacred literary locations is about connecting with a legacy that transcends generations. Through Lucy Maud Montgomery's writings, we glimpse the charm, wit, and intelligence of an imaginative girl navigating life in the late 19th century.

This legacy is a celebration of sorts, touching the hearts of millions across the globe and continuing to inspire despite generational gaps. One can almost see Montgomery and Anne at these historical sites, and hear their imaginative chatter, uplifting each other's spirits as well as those around them.

Since we are exploring her literary trail, it is interesting to highlight here the creative process or sources of inspiration Montgomery drew from when writing her Anne books. These were as follows:

- **Nature:** Montgomery's love for nature and writing seem to be deeply intertwined, both being great passions of hers. The stunning landscapes of PEI, with its rolling hills, magnificent forests, trails, and vast ocean views infused her writing with vivid imagery.
- **Personal journals:** She kept detailed journals, having started journaling at the young age of 9. In these journals, she revealed her struggles, ambitions, and insights into her emotional depth.

- **Real-life figures:** Many of the characters in *Anne of Green Gables* were inspired by people she knew in Cavendish, which makes her beloved Anne books even more realistic and intriguing.
- **Themes of belonging and identity:** The themes in her Anne books reflect important aspects of both her personal and literary journey. Like Anne, Montgomery sought belonging and was on a quest to experience deep personal fulfillment.

It is now time to take out your pencil and notepad—or use a notes app or blank document—whatever you prefer. The goal is to make some notes and add the following wonderful sites to your list of things to see, do, and explore in PEI and elsewhere. I have also included some additional sites to explore in Ontario, where Lucy spent time. Consider it a bonus and a good excuse to visit Ontario, another popular Montgomery tourist destination.

1. Prince Edward Island: The Heart of Her Imagination

Montgomery's Birthplace (Clifton)

There's a charming museum located in the village of New London, formerly known as Clifton. This, again, is where Montgomery was born. There are personal artifacts to look at, first editions of her books, and memorabilia from her childhood. You will also see her wedding dress and accessories on display.

Here, you will find some of her scrapbooks from her life as a student at Prince of Wales College, as well as from her years both as a writer and teacher. What is also fascinating at this museum is to see the old-fashioned furniture on display, such as a Franklin stove and an organ that belonged to her relatives.

There are many more artifacts to explore and lots to see in New London.

Cavendish (Green Gables Heritage Place)

We've already covered the iconic Green Gables Heritage Place in Chapter 1. So, mark it down, and be sure to make a stop there. Bring along your best walking shoes to ensure that you're as comfortable as possible. Throw in your sunhat and shades, and make up a picnic basket, so that you can stroll through Lover's Lane and the Haunted Wood with refreshments on hand.

Cavendish Cemetery

Still in Cavendish, you can visit the cemetery near Green Gables, where Lucy Maud Montgomery is buried alongside members of her family. This site attracts pilgrims from around the world who come to pay their respects and reflect on her remarkable literary contributions.

When Montgomery passed away in 1942, it was initially reported that she had succumbed to heart failure. However, her granddaughter, Kate Macdonald Butler, later revealed that Montgomery had taken an overdose of drugs and expressed remorse in a note left by her bedside (*L. M. Montgomery Suicide Revealed*, 2008).

It was speculated that she had been suffering from depression after years of caring for her mentally ill husband. Butler lifted the secrecy surrounding her death on the 100th anniversary of the publication of *Anne of Green Gables*. She did so to remove the stigma associated with mental health.

Montgomery's last words were captured in her suicide note, which read briefly as follows, "I have lost my mind by spells and I do not dare think what I may do in those spells. May God forgive me and I hope everyone else will forgive me even if they cannot understand" (Fasick 2021).

2. Leaskdale, Ontario: A New Chapter

Lucy Maud Montgomery Manse

The manse in Leaskdale is where Lucy Maud Montgomery lived for 15 years. In case you're wondering, a manse is the official residence provided to ministers, usually in the Christian faith. Such homes often have historical or architectural significance.

Montgomery married Ewan Macdonald on July 15th, 1911, after a lengthy courtship, and they settled in Ontario. Initially, she was unhappy in her marriage, stating, "I sat at that gay bridal feast, in my white veil and orange blossoms, beside the man that I had married—and I was as unhappy as I had ever been in my life" (Krzewinski, n.d.).

Eventually, she became more content with married life and had two sons. However, unhappiness resurfaced later on. Although they remained together for the rest of their lives, Ewan struggled with depression and a series of nervous breakdowns, placing a significant emotional burden on Montgomery.

You can gain a firsthand glimpse into her married life at the manse, which is now a National Historic Site.

Historic Leaskdale Church

Close to the manse, you can explore the historic church where Lucy Maud Montgomery's husband served as minister. There are guided tours available at the church. These tours reveal captivating stories about Montgomery's life and her lasting contributions to the local community. On the south side of the Church, there is a beautiful sculpture of Montgomery. Both in the house and church there are photographs of her and write-ups about her life.

3. Bala, Muskoka, Ontario

Bala's Museum With Memories of Lucy Maud Montgomery

In 1922, Montgomery and her family took a small vacation in the town of Bala, Muskoka, Ontario. During this time, she began daydreaming of a different adventure and wrote her book, *The Blue Castle*, her first novel set entirely outside of Prince Edward Island.

Although this historic site is located outside of PEI, it deserves mention. This is because it represents a significant acknowledgment of her contributions. As one learns more about Montgomery's struggles for recognition as a writer during her lifetime, it becomes clear that honoring her with museums in locations related to her literary accomplishments is justified.

Like many women writers of the early 20th century, Montgomery was not fully accepted by the Canadian literary community until after her death. Today, Montgomery is the biggest tourist draw to PEI. Some say she is the real force behind the island's tourism industry. The Bala Museum represents another way to pay tribute to this literary legend and serves as a tourist attraction in its own right.

It was established to honor the significance of her vacation there and her inspirational contributions to literature. *The Blue Castle* is set in Deerwood, another fictional town. However, there are clues in the book that suggest Deerwood is located in Bala and the Muskoka region, where Montgomery vacationed with her family.

They stayed at the Roselawn Cottage in Bala, which is now the museum itself.

Other Key Museums and Heritage Sites Dedicated to Her Work

Anne of Green Gables Museum (Park Corner, PEI)

This museum is nestled in the historic Campbell family homestead, who are relatives of Montgomery. The homestead inspired Montgomery's later novels, *Silver Bush* and *Pat of Silver Bush*. Located in Park Corner, it was built by Montgomery's Aunt Annie and Uncle John Campbell, who embodied the qualities of Matthew Cuthbert.

Here, you will find Anne's enchanted bookcase, which housed her imaginary friend, Katie Maurice. Another artifact on display is the organ that played during her wedding march. Additional items include Montgomery's Crazy Patchwork Quilt, the Blue Chest from *The Story Girl*, and much more. Nearby is the Lake of Shining Waters, where you can take a picture or relax and enjoy a picnic.

Now that you have explored the main sites that highlight significant aspects of her life and literary journey, it is time to turn our attention to food and all the delicious local cuisine that awaits you on your visit to PEI.

"Dear old world," she murmured, "you are very lovely, and I am glad to be alive in you."

–ANNE SHIRLEY

Chapter 7

Practical Travel Tips

The above-spirited words of Anne Shirley Cuthbert speak volumes about her impact on PEI tourism. Her love for this idyllic setting was all the more poignant given her earlier experiences of isolation in an uncaring asylum and foster home, making her arrival at Green Gables a transformative chapter in her life.

Finally, she was able to explore freely, unencumbered by tedious chores laid upon her by caregivers who always saw her as an outsider. When Green Gables and Avonlea became her home, PEI became a land of possibilities. It was no longer a trap, a prison of sorts stifling her curiosity and growth.

Keep in mind, though, that her imaginative creator was already deeply romanticizing her surroundings in Cavendish. Modern in outlook yet rooted in the comforting familiarity of her home, Montgomery masterfully wove tales that intertwined the beauty of Prince Edward Island with her beloved protagonist. All she ever wanted was to be recognized as a brilliant writer.

Well, she got so much more than that because today, PEI is inextricably linked with her legacy and the vivid, enchanting descriptions of its landscape.

The Importance of Historical Tours

If you search on the internet for fun things to do in PEI, Anne Shirley, Green Gables, and Lucy Maud Montgomery always pop up as key tourism highlights. This is what makes this book so important. The history of any place always attracts attention. Naturally, people want to explore what makes a place intriguing, charming, and unique.

Montgomery and her literary history are closely woven into the history of PEI, so much so that people plan their trips to PEI and Cavendish around festivals and Green Gable seasonal highlights. For example, even though summer and fall are excellent times to visit, Christmas at Green Gables is quite spectacular too.

Winter opening hours are limited, so if you don't want to miss this, be sure to check the Parks Canada website for details. You will find many kindred spirits at Green Gables during the Christmas season. The best part is that the surroundings are made up to resemble the late 19th century. Of course, Anne will be there too, greeting all her guests, and making sure that everyone feels right at home. There are plenty of cookies to decorate and lots of other fun things to do for the entire family. The best time to visit Green Gables depends on what you want to experience in PEI.

Alternatively, if you're interested in experiencing Avonlea in full bloom, then you should opt for a summer visit. Either way, you will still learn about the Macneills and how they found their way to this magical island from Scotland in the early 19th century, buying that piece of land that today is marked as a national heritage site of Canada.

So, history does count for something. In some instances, it makes the whole island an exciting and splendid thing to encounter. Truly, Anne and Montgomery are both compelling reasons to visit PEI at any time of the year.

The Best Times to Visit PEI

There truly is so much to look forward to when you plan your next vacation on PEI! Let's get started with the details.

In the Summertime (June to August)

If you love summer, then June to August is the best time to head over to PEI. It is the island's peak season, and you will enjoy plenty of beach island adventures during this time. The warm weather and festival season make this a big tourist draw.

It's a wonderful time to explore the red sand beaches, carefree and warm from the sun. Seafood is also abundant during the summer. From lobsters to mussels and oysters, there will be plenty of great offerings throughout the island. Let's just say, if you're a seafood lover, then PEI is a seafood paradise!

The island waters are awash in crab, lobster, shrimp, clams, and many types of fish. PEI can be a one-of-a-kind holiday for Anne fans, nature lovers, and seafood lovers. While it may be the smallest province in Canada, it is certainly one of the most enchanting places in the world, with exotic features to explore today.

In total, there are only 10 locations in the world where there are red-sand beaches. Cavendish is one of these 10. It is truly a jewel on its own. Of course, throughout the island, you will find both red and white sand beaches, but Cavendish is by far the prettiest and most popular, made famous by its red sand, and, of course, beloved red-haired Anne.

There are also vibrant summer festivals to look forward to, like the Cavendish Beach Music Festival, the Sommo Festival (which celebrates music, food, and drink), and the Festival of Small Halls (bringing music to smaller venues). There are lots of music festivities during the summer, which include food and drink at most venues. It is truly a vibrant time to be on the island during the peak season. You can add the following items to your bucket list for summer in PEI:

- **Get a scoop of Cowie Wowie:** This is a popular choice for tourists, especially in the summer when everyone is cheering on their favorite ice cream flavor. Try out Cows Creamery ice cream for yourself. It's the most famous ice cream on the island.
- **Take a cool stroll on the Cavendish Boardwalk:** This is a shoppers' paradise because there are many specialty shops here that offer just about everything, including comfortable summer fashion, unique gift ideas, souvenirs, and so much more.
- **Go for a ride at Sandspit:** This is a classic amusement park with more than 15 carnival favorites. They cater to all ages, so this is good fun for everyone.
- **Go see a show at the Confederation Center of the Arts:** Enjoy musicals, art, dance, and theater. This is good entertainment for everyone.
- **Spend a day at the Prince Edward Island National Park:** This is situated on the north shore and is best known for its lovely sandy beaches.

Be on the lookout for vibrant festivals and their highlights once you are on the island. There is never a dull moment during summer in PEI. Dress for summer, and pack layers of beach wear, casual clothes, walking shoes, and hiking gear! Throw in your sunhat, shades, and beach sandals.

During the Fall (September to October)

The air is crisp and cool, and the crowds are smaller. Still, you can have yourself quite an adventure during fall. The cool autumn air is crisp and inviting. This makes it a perfect time to explore forests and other exciting nature trails.

The foliage is especially stunning during the fall season, and the atmosphere is more peaceful, calm, and quieter—not as vibrant as the summertime, but still wonderful. Anne loved Octobers, remember? It feels like most people in PEI love fall, too, judging from their exciting line-up of things to do. Here are some fall events to keep in mind when planning your trip:

- **Moonlight Bazaar:** This takes place at the end of September on Victorian Row. Enjoy a night of music, fun, art, and delicious food under the full moon. The best part is that it is completely free to attend.
- **Farm Day in the City:** For some people, this is the best day of the year. It is usually held on October 6th, and the venue is downtown Charlottetown. Farm Day transforms Charlottetown into a fall-flavored oasis. It's colorful and lively with artisans, musicians, and food vendors all lined up. It is the biggest street festival of the year.
- **PEI's Oktoberfest:** Get ready to come on October 5th because that's when PEI hosts its Oktoberfest.

There's lots of German food on offer here, as well as live music, games, and great beers to go around.

- **Halloween night:** Be ready for a good and unusual scare on Halloween in Kensington. This is a thrilling time for visitors who love Halloween. You can test your nerve for thrills at the haunted mansion which overlooks Kensington. The mansion was built in 1890 and it is believed to be haunted.
- **Fall flavors:** This is a food and drink festival that celebrates Canada's Food Island. Unique events are hosted in unique venues, and all of them feature delicious food prepared with local ingredients. It is usually held from September 26th until October 12th.
- **The Charlottetown Scarecrow Festival:** This is one of the most fun events of the year. Scarecrows take to the streets in Charlottetown during the fall, reminding everyone of the new season, and creating a festive atmosphere. This is a month-long festival that is held during October and should not be missed. It is truly one of a kind.

Now that you have a good idea of how fabulous it is to visit in autumn, there's no excuse for thinking that it will only be fun in summer! It all depends on what you want to experience. Be prepared for rainy weather, though, as well as cool evenings. The weather is changeable and it does get quite cold. So pack jackets, some warmer clothing, and a few long-sleeved shirts. Make sure that your shoes are comfortable for walking, too.

In the Winter (December to February)

While chilly, winter is magical for those seeking solitude or activities like snowshoeing and cozy evenings by the fire. Don't be fooled into thinking that island fun stops during the winter. There's a lot to keep you enjoying PEI during this season. Here are some of the highlights:

- **Winterdine:** This happens in downtown Charlottetown. It is a winter festival of sorts with 20 participating restaurants. Each of these restaurants offers multiple-course meals. It all depends on the restaurant and what you want to eat. Give your taste buds a treat on a winter budget and sample some of Charlottetown's best cuisine.

- **Winter Festival:** Immerse yourself in the winter wonderland of Points East Coastal Drive. There, you can enjoy sledding, skating, and snowshoeing.

- **Winter Warmth Festival:** The Winter Warmth Festival in Summerside is designed to warm the body, mind, and spirit. It consists of culinary events, skating, biking, snowshoeing, and seaside fun.

- **Ice City Festival:** There's so much to enjoy here. Activities include ice skating, sculpting, and even horse and wagon rides. This festival is held in Charlottetown.

These are only some of the highlights to look forward to in winter. Keep in mind that winter snow storms are quite common in PEI, so dress up warmly, and take along your snowshoes, hat, gloves, and layers of warm clothing. Imagine that you're stepping into a winter wonderland in PEI!

It's Springtime (April to May)

Spring offers mild weather and blooming landscapes. It is also an ideal season to explore the island. You can beat the crowds and get so much out of your PEI trip. Spring is a joyous time on the island because it marks the start of all the festivals. It's also lobster season in PEI! Here are some of the island's spring highlights:

- **Visit the lighthouses:** In total, there are 63 lighthouses in PEI and spring is a great time to visit some of them and learn more about the history of the island. Most of them date back to Anne's days. Visitors enjoy the lighthouse tours because they're historic. Make it a point to spend a day visiting them, and you will not be disappointed.
- **Trails:** This is a great season for hiking, biking, walking, and exploring more nature trails. The weather is warmer and locals tend to spend as much time outdoors as possible.
- **Play Golf:** You can head off to the golf course near Green Gables, but there are plenty of other golf clubs on the island too.
- **Restaurants:** Since it's lobster season, you can enjoy plenty of them during the spring. All across the island,

restaurants serve plenty of seafood. Take your pick in Cavendish, Kensington, or Charlottetown.

- **The Charlottetown Farmers Market:** This is a wonderful way to spend a Saturday spring morning. There's a lot to soak in while you enjoy the music, artwork, and food on sale here. Many say this market offers the most authentic PEI food and cultural experience.

Once again, these are only some of the highlights. Since you already know how beautiful the landscape is from Montgomery's writing, you can rightly anticipate beautiful warm weather, which also makes it ideal for spending longer hours on the red-sand beaches. Dress lightly, pack shorter-sleeved cardigans, dresses, and beachwear, and carry a light jacket for cooler evening temperatures.

Suggested Itineraries for Different Lengths of Stay

1–2 Days: An Anne-Centric Escape

For a brief escape to PEI, you can spend your time in Cavendish exploring the wonderful world of Anne at the Green Gables Heritage Place, as well as nearby sites like Avonlea Village, which is tied to the Anne books and Montgomery's life. Walk the Haunted Wood and Lover's Lane trails to experience the landscapes that inspired her, and visit both Montgomery's birthplace and her Cavendish home, as each is within a short drive. In the evening, reflect on your day with a traditional lobster supper or a quiet moment watching the sunset at one of the stunning nearby beaches.

3–5 Days: Anne and Beyond

For a slightly longer visit, enjoy a reflection of Anne's world and the broader charm of Prince Edward Island. Spend two full days in Cavendish immersing yourself in the Anne-related sites. Thereafter, immerse yourself in the natural world of PEI by enjoying time at the Prince Edward Island National Park with its stunning coastal views and beaches. On another day, take a scenic drive along one of the island's coastal routes—North Cape Coastal Drive or Points East Coastal Drive. You can stop at lighthouses, artisan shops, and fishing villages. Then, finally in Charlottetown, visit the Confederation Center of the Arts, which celebrates PEI's literary and cultural heritage. Finish it off with a lovely meal at a waterfront restaurant.

7 Days or More: A Full Island Experience

A week or longer will give you the chance to fully immerse yourself in Anne's world while also experiencing the island's natural beauty and culture. Dedicate at least three days to Cavendish and its Anne-related sites. Relax on nearby beaches and explore nature trails. Since you have more time, you can spend some of it outdoors soaking in the beauty and charm of PEI. Enjoy picnics and take lots of photos. You can also extend your exploration of Charlottetown, the South Shore, and some off-the-beaten-path areas.

Try water activities like kayaking or deep-sea fishing, sample the island's renowned culinary delights, and embrace PEI's slower pace of life. With these itineraries, your trip to Prince Edward Island can be as magical and memorable as Anne's adventures in Avonlea.

Now that you've seen how to craft your dream PEI escape, you're ready to start your journey. In the next chapter, we will reflect on Anne's enduring legacy before I bid you *bon voyage*!

I'm not a bit changed—not really. I'm only just pruned down and branched out. The real ME—back here—is just the same.

–ANNE SHIRLEY

Chapter 8

Reflections on Anne's Legacy

Anne's popularity has remained widespread for more than a century since she caught the world's attention. Without a doubt, there's so much to Anne that keeps people in awe of her journey to this day. She is warm-hearted, witty, and down-to-earth. Her character serves as a poignant reminder of those things that are meaningful in life and Anne, of course, constantly reminds us of the importance of acknowledging endless possibilities and happy endings.

Her trials and tribulations resonate deeply with most of us because they reflect universal struggles, such as the desire to belong, and to do something amazing with our lives. Young women, especially, are likely to relate deeply to Anne's emotional struggles because she highlights them so profoundly.

There's also the universal need to find one's place in the world. Both Anne and Montgomery desire nothing more than to establish a firm foothold in their chosen careers. In her era, Montgomery's portrayal of Anne as an independent and determined girl and woman was groundbreaking. But even today, the idea of women having an equal chance of achieving the same greatness as men is still sadly frowned upon in certain societies and cultures.

This is what makes Anne a timeless role model for girls and women everywhere. Anne's sharp intelligence and unique way of thinking and expressing herself are truly captivating. Interestingly, the fact that Anne's story is set in the late 19th century adds an enchanting layer to its appeal. Anne's deep love for the natural world reignites in readers a sense of wonder and appreciation for its beauty.

There's no denying the charm of the late 19th-century lifestyle. The lively small-town festivals bring people together to enjoy activities like baking contests and community gatherings. PEI, with its vibrant festivals and picturesque nature trails, embodies the charm of late 19th-century Avonlea, continuing to inspire the world. This enduring influence is also Anne's legacy.

Above all, there's virtue in rebelliousness if it brings about transformation!

The Various Adaptations of Anne of Green Gables

Numerous adaptations of *Anne of Green Gables* exist today. The novel continues to inspire feature films, stage productions, television series adaptations, animations, and musicals. Every adaptation is unique and has brought something new to the story. However, they all maintain the essence of Anne and include the most famous scenes and dialogue from the novel.

While the 1985 CBC miniseries starring Megan Follows as Anne Shirley is often considered the most beloved adaptation by fans due to its faithfulness to the original novel, *Anne With an E*—a coproduction for CBC and Netflix—contains a modern charm, and is seen by many as just as compelling as the 1985 adaptation. Keep in mind, though, that it's been often labeled a "darker version" of the novel due to its modern themes and choice to tackle issues such as gender inequality, racism, class discrimination, and mental health.

Indeed, *Anne With an E* places more emphasis on Anne's mental health following a traumatic childhood dominated by abuse and neglect as an orphan. This adaptation therefore portrays Anne as an unstable child struggling with PTSD and identity issues. Anne comes across as being more vulnerable and emotionally challenged by her past. Still, the adaptation maintains the iconic charm of the novel and the wholesome, nourishing values that exist side by side with 19th-century gender and racial issues.

Beyond these adaptations, Anne continues to inspire fan communities globally—and we know already that PEI is a pilgrimage destination for Anne fans.

Anne Shirley as a Symbol of Empowerment and Resilience

Anne's story highlights the struggle of the marginalized to rise above prejudice and societal biases to claim their rightful place in the world. This is how Anne becomes a symbol of empowerment for others. She exudes the traits of someone who feels worthy of life, as well as worthy of chasing her dreams regardless of the opinions of anyone else.

The qualities she exudes happen to be the same ones that Dr. Carol Dweck suggests are important for growth. According to Dr. Dweck, a growth mindset is the ultimate ticket to ensuring prolonged growth and success in life, based on the premise that abilities and intelligence can be developed through dedication and hard work (*Decades of Scientific Research*, 2017).

We see those qualities in Anne as she refuses to give in to the narrow-mindedness of people like the critical Rachel Lynde, the petty Josie Pye, or the skeptical Mrs. Barry, who represent the societal prejudices Anne faces in the community of Avonlea. She works hard in school to earn her acceptance to Queen's Academy and is therefore afforded a chance in life to reach her highest potential, which has nothing to do with being an orphan girl.

In the late 19th century, women with progressive traits were often seen as rebellious and unfavorably labeled "feminist" or "troublesome" by those who upheld patriarchal values that excluded women from advancing in society. Including women in world affairs was widely frowned upon during that era, making Montgomery's achievement with Anne truly remarkable.

Finally, Anne's empowerment is reflected in her relationship with other women, mainly Marilla Cuthbert. As we've touched on before, Marilla serves as a mentor figure who helps Anne navigate the complexities of adulthood. Yet, she also transforms to adapt to Anne's more progressive ways. She starts seeing through the veil of rebelliousness in Anne and notices that beyond all of that is a girl who dares to follow her heart and pursue some truly inspiring goals. As a result, Marilla grows more accepting of Anne and her ways and offers her genuine support and love.

This can serve as a reminder of the importance of offering love and support to others who desire to prosper in life. More than just being a literary classic, the story of *Anne of Green Gables* shines as a celebration of resilience and determination, inspiring us to rise above challenges and embrace the potential within us all.

CONCLUSION

Anne Shirley will always be deeply associated with Prince Edward Island, the most beloved place of her creator, Lucy Maud Montgomery. Montgomery's ability to bring Anne to life in this beautiful setting, closely connected to her reality, makes Avonlea feel real to us, allowing us to imagine PEI in all its vivid beauty. Her gift means that those who have chosen to follow *In the Footsteps of Anne* by traveling to PEI may feel as if they've already been there.

In the Footsteps of Anne also has attempted to reflect on the remarkable relationships that Anne developed and nurtured in Avonlea. Each connection she forges helps shape her into a compassionate, thoughtful, and determined woman, just as the connections in our lives shape our identities to some degree.

Anne and her creator, affectionately known as Lucy Maud among islanders, are similar in many ways and remain dear to PEI—and the world beyond it. Indeed, fans cherish them for their enormous contributions all over the globe. Their stories and lives are intertwined with the history of PEI, transforming it into a vibrant tourist hub.

The official tourism website for PEI states that as far back as 1908, people have traveled to PEI to visit the magical setting of

Anne of Green Gables—millions of them, in fact (Anne of Green Gables, n.d.).

PEI would not be what it is today without Anne and her wonderful ways. It's truly remarkable to think about this. The way Anne has touched lives and continues to inspire kindred spirits to visit the island is something to marvel at, demonstrating the powerful impact that one's imagination can have on the world. This imagination has led many Anne enthusiasts to the island for various reasons, but none simpler than this: Anne makes us feel good.

As a red-haired girl who always felt a bit out of place, *Anne of Green Gables* was a gift to me in childhood. I related to Anne's dislike of her fiery hair, her vivid imagination, and the way she seemed to stumble through life with the best of intentions. Much like Anne, I often felt like I didn't quite fit in with the world around me. She was a kindred spirit. Her story gave me comfort, showing me that it was okay to be different, to dream big, and to embrace my quirks—whether they stemmed from my hair color, my freckles, or my tendency to talk a little too much.

Anne's ability to turn every setback into an opportunity for growth was something I held on to as I navigated my challenges, finding strength in her resilience and determination. Growing up, I was often told I talked too much, just like Anne, and I confess to spending some time sitting alone in the school hall as punishment for my incessant chatter!

In Anne, I saw a reflection of my voice—loud and full of stories, bursting with ideas and opinions. She reminded me that having a lot to say wasn't a fault; it was a gift. Anne's words, her relentless enthusiasm, and her colorful way of viewing the world resonated with me. She proved that being yourself, no matter how much you might feel like a misfit, could lead to the most extraordinary life.

As I've grown older, the story of Anne and Avonlea remains a touchstone for me, something that has stayed with me through the years. The village of Avonlea, with its close-knit community and a rich sense of place, has become a symbol of the belonging I longed for as a child and has fueled my lifelong quest to settle in a smaller, simpler place.

Avonlea is where the unconventional is celebrated, where individuality is prized, and where love, friendship, and loyalty run deep—qualities that now guide me. Anne shows us that it's not only okay to embrace your uniqueness; it's something to be cherished. The story of Anne, in all its whimsy and wisdom, remains a beacon for living an authentic life.

I hope you have enjoyed walking *In the Footsteps of Anne* as much as I have enjoyed putting this book together, inspired by my visits to PEI and the richness of the lives of both Lucy Maud Montgomery and Anne Shirley Cuthbert. Together, we have traveled to Green Gables, where the apple orchards planted by Montgomery's grandfather, Alexander Macneill, still produce beautiful blossoms each year.

It's amazing to contemplate how splendidly Montgomery blended reality with fiction. What was beloved to her while growing up on the Macneill Farm was also cherished by Anne. For Montgomery, Green Gables represents a happier childhood, bringing greater harmony to the beauty she sees from her window. We can imagine that the same sweet-scented floral smells that drifted up to Anne's bedroom at Green Gables filled Lucy Maud with joy as she wrote and described Anne's first morning in Avonlea.

The Lake of Shining Waters, the White Way of Delight, Lover's Lane, and the Haunted Wood all remain dear to readers and viewers of the Anne stories, well preserved and treasured. The places you discovered in this book symbolize the heartfelt connections and memories we share with the people of Avonlea. Anne's story continues to open hearts and minds, influencing generations of people from all walks of life.

I urge you to read the Anne books again or watch your favorite TV adaptation. If you are planning a trip to PEI, mark your favorite scenes and aspire to truly walk in Anne's footsteps, reimagining them in your mind and feeling touched all over again by her remarkable way of expressing joy.

Both Anne and Montgomery share important lessons about life, teaching us, above all else, the significance of following one's heart and dreams. Montgomery pursued her passion to be a writer and, against all odds, succeeded despite the setbacks, heartbreaks, and limited opportunities for girls and women in that era.

Anne's spirit is contagious, her words filled with awe and wisdom for both young and old alike. Let Anne's spirit inspire your daily life. There is potential in everyday moments and magic in nature, but only if we allow ourselves to connect with life in a certain way—in Anne's way. So, let this be her gift to you. May Lucy Maud Montgomery's Anne remain a treasured companion on your own life's journey, and may you find inspiration as you make the trek to Avolea and truly walk *in the footsteps of Anne*.

REFERENCES

Anne of Green Gables. (n.d.). Tourism PEI. https://www.tourismpei.com/what-to-do/anne-of-green-gables

Basin Head Provincial Park. (n.d.). Tourism PEI. https://www.tourismpei.com/what-to-do/beaches-parks/basin-head-provincial-park

Brecknell, M. (2024, November 27). *The troubled life of L. M. Montgomery*. Early Bird Books. https://earlybirdbooks.com/lm-montogomery-biography

Cavendish-North Rustico. (2024). Parks Canada. https://parks.canada.ca/pn-np/pe/pei-ipe/visit/cavendish-nr

Decades of scientific research started a growth mindset revolution. (2017). Mindsetworks. https://www.mindsetworks.com/science/

Fasick, A. (2021, November 28). *Happy books and a sad life*. Teacups and Tyrants. https://teacupsandtyrants.com/2021/11/28/happy-books-and-a-sad-life-lucy-maud-montgomery/

Feminism in the 19th century. (2016, January 8). Atria. https://institute-genderequality.org/news-publications/feminism/feminism-19th-century/

Fun and festive PEI Fall. (2024, December). Welcome PEI. https://welcomepei.com/editorial/a-fun-and-festive-pei-fall/

Green. (2022, April 19). *L. M. Montgomery (1874–1942): A writer's creative life*. The Anne of Green Gables Manuscript: https://annemanuscript.ca/stories/a-writers-life/

Green Gables Christmas. (2024). World of Anne Shirley. https://www.worldofanneshirley.com/2024/11/a-green-gables-christmas.html

Green Gables Heritage Place. (2023, March 16). Parks.canada.ca. https://parks.canada.ca/lhn-nhs/pe/greengables

Green Gables House. (2019). Parks Canada. https://www.pc.gc.ca/apps/dfhd/page_fhbro_eng.aspx?id=2491

The haunted wood trail at Green Gables Heritage Place. (2024). Worldofanneshirley. https://www.worldofanneshirley.com/2007/07/the-haunted-wood-trail.html

Hogan, M. (2022, March 29). *101 Things to Do in PEI (2023 Hand-picked Guide)*. Suitcase and Heels. https://suitcaseandheels.com/101-things-to-do-in-pei/

The House of Home. (2022, February 23). The Anne of Green Gables Manuscript. https://annemanuscript.ca/stories/the-house-of-home/

Krzewinski, A. (n.d.). *Lucy Maud Montgomery's varied love life*. Road to Avonlea. https://www.roadtoavonlea.com/blog-posts/lucy-maud-montgomerys-varied-love-life

L. M. Montgomery's suicide revealed. (2008, September 22). CBC. https://www.cbc.ca/news/canada/prince-edward-island/l-m-montgomery-suicide-revealed-1.723426

Long River United Church. (2024). *Blogspot*. https://peiheritagebuildings.blogspot.com/2011/08/long-river-united-church.html

Lucy Maud Montgomery. (2024). The Canadian Encyclopedia. https://www.thecanadianencyclopedia.ca/en/article/lucy-maud-montgomery-plain-language-summary

Lucy Maud Montgomery Poems. (2019). Poem Hunter. https://www.poemhunter.com/lucy-maud-montgomery/

Lucy Maud Montgomery's inspiring trip to Bala, Ontario in 1922. (2023, February 21). Typepad. https://torontopubliclibrary.typepad.com/local-history-genealogy/2023/02/lucy-maud-montgomerys-inspiring-trip-to-bala-ontario-in-1922.html

The Manse. (2011, March 31). Lucy Maud Montgomery Society of Ontario. https://lucymaudmontgomery.ca/tours/the-manse/

McIntosh, A., & Devereux, C. (2013, January 1). *Lucy Maud Montgomery.* The Canadian encyclopedia.ca. https://www.thecanadianencyclopedia.ca/en/article/montgomery-lucy-maud

McNeill, Bell, MacMillan, Munn, Ma. (2024). Genealogy. https://www.genealogy.com/forum/regional/countries/topics/canada/princeedwardisland/511/

Montgomery, L. (n.d.). *Anne of Green Gables quotes.* Goodreads. https://www.goodreads.com/work/quotes/3464264-anne-of-green-gables

Montgomery, L. M. (1908). *Anne of Green Gables.* Grosset & Dunlap.

Montgomery, L. M. (2022, May 23). Anne of Green Gables quotes. Scary Mommy. https://www.scarymommy.com/entertainment/anne-of-green-gable-quotes

Montgomery, L. M. (2024). *Anne of Green Gables quotes.* Goodreads. https://www.goodreads.com/quotes/79687-we-pay-a-price-for-everything-we-get-or-take

Shubic, M. (2017, December 5). *A guide to a Prince Edward Island road trip.* Mike's Road Trip. https://mikesroadtrip.com/pei-road-trip-guide/

Thirty things to do this winter in Prince Edward Island. (2024, January 4). To Do Canada. https://www.todocanada.ca/25-things-winter-prince-edward-island/

The ultimate guide to Prince Edward Island for fans of Anne of Green Gables. (2019, January 18). Gone with the Family.

https://www.gonewiththefamily.com/2019/01/anne-of-green-gables-prince-edward-island.html

Who was Lucy Maud Montgomery? (n.d.). The Famous People. https://www.thefamouspeople.com/profiles/lucy-maud-montgomery-3961.php

Image References

Albert, S. (2018). *Horses-carriage-horse-3628030.* [Image]. Pixabay. https://pixabay.com/photos/horses-carriage-horse-l%C3%BCneburg-heath-3628030/

Amber, M. (2018). *Meadow-farmhouse-trees-fence-gate-3169294.* [Image]. Pixabay. https://pixabay.com/photos/meadow-farmhouse-trees-fence-gate-3169294/

Avenue-trees-tree-lined-path-trail-2215317. (2017). [Image]. Pixabay. https://pixabay.com/photos/avenue-trees-tree-lined-path-trail-2215317/

Beach-sand-shore-nature-sea-ocean-8268375. (2023). [Image]. Pixabay. https://pixabay.com/photos/beach-sand-shore-nature-sea-ocean-8268375/

Board-slate-blackboard-chalk-1614646. (2016). [Image]. Pixabay. https://pixabay.com/photos/board-slate-blackboard-chalk-1614646/

Bode, R., & Mitchell, J. (2018). *L.M. Montgomery and the matter of nature(s).* McGillQueen's University Press. https://doi.org/10.2307/j.ctv8j5dh

Books-reading-bedroom-bed-2619265. (2017). [Image]. Pixabay. https://pixabay.com/photos/books-reading-bedroom-bed-2619265/

Bornem, B. (2016). *Reading-book-girl-read-summer-1500650.* [Image]. Pixabay. https://pixabay.com/photos/reading-book-girl-read-summer-1500650/

Brown, T. (2022). *Landscape-tree-nature-forest-7284515.* [Image]. Pixabay. https://pixabay.com/photos/landscape-tree-nature-forest-7284515/

Causby, D. (2017). *Prince-edward-island-pei-canada-2733569.* [Image]. Pixabay. https://pixabay.com/photos/prince-edward-island-pei-canada-2733569/

Duang, X. (2023). *Camping-picnic-lunch-dining-travel-7947056.* [Image]. Pixabay. https://pixabay.com/photos/camping-picnic-lunch-dining-travel-7947056/

E, R. (2016). *Window-flower-the-atmosphere-out-1594287.* [Image]. Pixabay. https://pixabay.com/photos/window-flower-the-atmosphere-out-1594287/

Ilyés, I. (2021). *Lake-forest-park-bench-tree-wood-6278825.* [Image]. Pixabay. https://pixabay.com/photos/lake-forest-park-bench-tree-wood-6278825/

Ivanovs, A. (2013). *Rail-railroad-countryside-railway-234318.* [Image]. Pixabay. https://pixabay.com/photos/rail-railroad-countryside-railway-234318/

Joy, F. (2017). *Anne-of-green-gables-portrait-2770442.* [Image]. Pixabay. https://pixabay.com/photos/anne-of-green-gables-portrait-2770442/

Jualita. (2018). *Everything-goes-autumn-sadness-3741141.* [Image]. Pixabay. https://pixabay.com/photos/everything-goes-autumn-sadness-3741141/

Lighthouse-prince-edward-island-6463769. (2021). [Image]. Pixabay. https://pixabay.com/photos/lighthouse-prince-edward-island-6463769/

Montani, G. (2018). *Desk-historical-antique-office-3606980.* [Image]. Pixabay. https://pixabay.com/photos/desk-historical-antique-office-3606980/

Nola. (2020). *Boat-shed-boat-prince-edward-island-5140491.* [Image]. Pixabay. https://pixabay.com/photos/boat-shed-boat-prince-edward-island-5140491/

Ovsyannykov, I. (2017). *Adult-asia-asian-bangkok-beautiful-2693054.* [Image]. Pixabay. https://pixabay.com/photos/adult-asia-asian-bangkok-beautiful-2693054/

P, N. (2020). *Boat-shed-boat-prince-edward-island-5140491*. [Image]. Pixabay. https://pixabay.com/photos/boat-shed-boat-prince-edward-island-5140491/

Tan, V. (2019). *Sweets-tea-snacks-lamp-tea-snack-4313400*. [Image]. Pixabay. https://pixabay.com/illustrations/sweets-tea-snacks-lamp-tea-snack-4313400/

Werner, B. (2012b). *Prince-edward-island-canada-54990*. [Image]. Pixabay. https://pixabay.com/photos/prince-edward-island-canada-54990/

Winkler, M. (2020). *Typewriter-female-empowerment-5519043*. [Image]. Pixabay. https://pixabay.com/photos/typewriter-female-empowerment-5519043/

Woman-farm-countryside-cropland-1851503. (2016). [Image]. Pixabay. https://pixabay.com/photos/woman-farm-countryside-cropland-1851503/

Printed in Great Britain
by Amazon

320c5c44-a5fc-4a5c-9d1c-9aebf30f0690R01